Goodbye London

An Illustrated Guide to Threatened Buildings

Christopher Booker and Candida Lycett Green

Fontana/Collins

First published in Fontana 1973
Copyright © Christopher Booker and Candida Lycett Green 1973

Maps by Oxford Illustrators

Typeset is originated by Filmtype Services Limited, Scarborough

Printed in Great Britain
by William Collins Sons & Co. Ltd, Glasgow

Contents

    Authors' note   4
    Abbreviations   4
    Introduction   6
    Historical Background   9
    Map of Conservation Areas in Central London   16
1   North-West Kensington   18
2   South Kensington and Chelsea   27
3   Paddington and Bayswater   39
4   North of Oxford Street   45
5   Soho   55
6   Mayfair   65
7   Victoria   71
8   Whitehall to Temple   81
9   Covent Garden   87
10   Bloomsbury and Camden   101
11   Kingsway to Ludgate Hill   109
12   The City   115
13   Southwark   133
14   Periphery   137
    Developers   144
    Architects   151
    Planners   156
    Listed Buildings and Conservation Areas   158
    The Role of the Public   158
    Suggestions   159

Authors' note

All the buildings listed in this text have been threatened with demolition, except where stated. This does not mean that demolition is certain. The planning situation is constantly changing. By the time this book comes out, some of these schemes may have been refused, some dropped, some altered and new ones will have been put forward.

Abbreviations

A   Architect
Ap Applicant
D   Developer
O   Owner
P   Proposal

Acknowledgments

Hundreds of people have helped us in the compilation of this book, and it is impossible to mention them all. But we would particularly like to thank the planning departments of the following councils for their patience with a mass of queries: Kensington and Chelsea, Westminster, Camden, the City, Southwark, Islington, Hammersmith, Tower Hamlets. Our thanks also to Ashley Barker and the Historic Buildings Board, Mr Croad of the National Monuments Record; the GLC Covent Garden Planning team; Jim Monahan of the Covent Garden Community; Peter Burman of the Council of Places for Worship; David Lloyd of the Victorian Society; the Kensington and other amenity societies; David Wilcox of the *Evening Standard*; Michael Hanson; Oliver Marriott's *The Property Boom*; and the *Investor's Review*.

A more personal debt of gratitude is due to Diana Keeley, Diana Crawfurd, Tessa Fantoni and Jean Hallman; also to Lydia Greeves, John Trevitt and Francis Bennett of Fontana for coping with various unusual problems; to Derek Boshier; particularly to Christine and Rupert; and lastly to Benita Egge.

Most of the pictures have been taken by the authors, but we are also grateful to Christopher Thynne, the Royal Commission on Historical Monuments, the GLC Historic Buildings Division and photograph library, Universal Press and Pictorial, the *Financial Times* Photo Library, *Building Design*, Baron Studios, Beaverbrook Newspapers and the *Middlesex Chronicle*.

Introduction

In the next ten years, the face of London could be changed more than at any other time in history.

Over recent months, some of the large redevelopment plans, such as Covent Garden and Piccadilly, have been widely discussed. But in fact these are only the tip of a giant iceberg of plans for re-building all over central London.

In this book, we have attempted to give some kind of overall picture of what is happening. We have tried to show what is being planned, thought about and otherwise seriously considered at the time the book goes to press, at the beginning of 1973.

Obviously on a subject so often surrounded with secrecy, there is much we may have missed. The situation is constantly changing. But to present as complete a picture as possible, we have consulted planning applications, press reports, authorities, developers, architects, landowners, estate plans and experts of all kinds.

Area covered
The area we have chosen is that normally regarded as central London. It stretches from the residential districts of Kensington and Chelsea on the west, through the City of Westminster and the southern half of Camden, to the City and Southwark on the east. This is the London that everybody knows. We have also included a few sites of exceptional interest outside this central area.

General note
It is not the purpose of this book to judge whether all the proposed developments are desirable or not. But too often in the past con-troversial schemes have come to public notice only after all the key decisions have been taken.

Among the reasons why the public have become increasingly concerned about redevelopment are:

Introduction

(1) The scale on which it is taking place.

(2) The fact that in the past fifteen years we have been introduced to an almost entirely new type of architecture, which not only makes a complete break with the London of the past, but is widely considered to be 'impersonal' and 'soulless'.

Much modern development seems to be an inescapable product of late 20th-century society. Old buildings lose their uses or become uneconomic. Modern buildings are often more comfortable and efficient to work in, and can make a striking addition to the landscape.

Nevertheless it cannot be denied that most modern building produces an architecture distinctly lacking in local character, so that not only do all parts of London come to look alike, but London itself becomes indistinguishable from almost any other major city in the world.

Another consequence of massive redevelopment in the past decade is that London office rents are now among the highest in the world — having risen from £1 a foot to £10 and upwards in 1972 (as compared with such figures as £4 in New York, £6.50 in Paris and £2.50 in Brussels). New buildings may be 'economically viable' for the developer; they are not always so for the user.

By no means all the buildings we have included are of beauty, but they are all familiar to someone. So much of the experience of living in, and feeling at home in a city is the familiar streetscape, the favourite area, the unexpected detail on a building, the shops one regularly uses. To anyone who lives in London, the past ten years have afforded a continuous unsettling and sometimes saddening experience of seeing such familiarity gradually eaten away.

All too often the result of this is the breaking up of a community. A group of people who had come to live and work together in familiar surroundings, over years and possibly generations, is dispersed. To record something of that is why we have written this book.

Historical Background

1580. The first attempt at London planning. In order to prevent
continued spread of the city, a Royal Proclamation prohibited building
on any site where a building had not stood in living memory.
Confirmed by Act of Parliament in 1592 and several times later,
these measures nevertheless failed to curb what many felt to be a
serious problem.

1630. The 4th Earl of Bedford commissioned Inigo Jones to redevelop 7 acres of Covent Garden, with church and piazza — London's
first square. The plan aroused furious opposition from the inhabitants,
who resented the destruction of their community and intimate-scale
Tudor houses. Other squares followed during the rest of the 17th
century: Leicester Square (1635), Soho Square (1681), St James's
Square (1684), Red Lion Square (1684), Grosvenor Square (1695),
and Berkeley Square (1698).

1666. Great Fire devastates the City. Wren's comprehensive
development plan, produced in ten days, thwarted by householders
already beginning to rebuild on their own sites.

1768. London's first instance of a major speculative development
scheme — the Adelphi. The Adam brothers leased the site of Durham
House and several acres of small, dilapidated houses between the
Strand and the river from the Duke of St Albans, and sunk their
fortune in a grand redevelopment, the centrepiece of which was the

*John Adam St: surviving fragments of
Adams' Adelphi scheme (1772)*

Goodbye London

Adelphi Terrace of 24 houses built on a brick-arched platform over the river. For a long time the Adams found great difficulty in disposing of the leases on their buildings, until they were saved by a special National Lottery, sanctioned by Parliament.

The Adam brothers were forerunners of today's speculative developers and architects in other respects. Lord Foley, who owned a mansion on the outskirts of London on the present site of the Langham Hotel (by the BBC), was persuaded to sell the land to the north of his house, but stipulated that it should not be built upon. The Adam brothers saw that the contract only stipulated that building should not take place on a line directly north of the house itself. They were thus free to build two terraces to the north of each side of the house. Lord Foley found his country residence suddenly surrounded with building on three sides; and the result was Portland Place.

1813–30. First major comprehensive redevelopment scheme — Nash's triumphal way from the Mall, via Regent St, to Regent's Park.

Left, the last remnant of Nash's Regent St; right, Regent St as it was

Large-scale compulsory purchase through the streets of west Soho made possible by Act of Parliament.

1824. Thomas Cubitt negotiated contracts with Duke of Bedford for large-scale redevelopment of north Bloomsbury, and Lord Grosvenor for building of squares and streets of Belgravia.

1845. Act of Parliament passed for construction of Victoria St, involving demolition of several celebrated old buildings, including 15th-century Caxton's House. New street was opened 1851, although it was many years before all sites were rebuilt.

1865. First stirrings of 'conservation movement'. Northumberland House, a fine Jacobean mansion at the south-east corner of Trafalgar

Historical Background

Square, was served with a compulsory purchase order by the Metropolitan Board of Works, for the construction of a new street joining Trafalgar Square and the Embankment. After vigorous protests the scheme was dropped, but successfully revived again in 1872. In 1874 the House was demolished, and Northumberland Avenue opened in 1876.

1877. Society for the Preservation of Ancient Buildings founded by William Morris. In 1875 the Society for Photographing Old London had been formed because so many ancient buildings were being demolished, such as the last remaining 16th-century galleried coaching inn in the City.

1873–90. Queen Anne's Mansions built by developer Henry Hankey, 151 ft high, and the tallest private building in London. So great was public outrage (including Queen Victoria, resentful at being overlooked in Buckingham Palace) that in 1888 the London Building Act was passed, limiting the height of buildings to 80ft, or the width of the street in which they stood. This restriction on height played a crucial part in the development of London over the next sixty years, until the provisions were relaxed in the 1950s.

1899. The Kingsway Scheme, new road between Holborn and the Strand, involving wholesale destruction of existing streets. But preservation of the two churches in the Strand showed growing awareness of the value of the past. Kingsway was opened in 1905, although the complete scheme, including the building of the Aldwych, was not finished until 1931.

1923–7. Destruction and redevelopment of Nash's Regent St.

1934. Plans for rebuilding of Nash's Carlton House Terrace by Sir Reginald Blomfield, architect of new Regent St Quadrant (later abandoned).

During the twenties and the thirties, major redevelopment took place in many parts of London, including the destruction of many of the famous aristocratic town houses (Norfolk House, Lansdowne House, Devonshire House, Dorchester House, Grosvenor House), 18th-century Grosvenor and Berkeley Squares, and in 1936 the demolition of the Adelphi Terrace. In their place rose large impersonal blocks of a new kind, such as those on Park Lane between the Dorchester and Grosvenor House, the BBC, Shell-Mex House, the Cumberland Hotel, the new Bank of England (replacing Sir John Soane's masterpiece of 1788–1810), the Freemason's Hall in Long Acre (200 ft) and the London University tower in Malet St (220 ft).

During the War, thousands more buildings were destroyed, including a third of the City. This gave impetus to a second great rebuilding programme after the War, and such rethinking as was symbolised by the Abercrombie Plan for the County of London published in 1943. This envisaged drastic road-widening and slum clearance schemes, and other proposals which have been the basis for much planning since, such as the redevelopment of the South Bank, and the moving of Covent Garden Market (although this was first suggested in 1926).

Goodbye London

POST-WAR DEVELOPMENT

The post-War history of London's redevelopment has been through four main phases, the fourth of which is just beginning.

First phase (1945–54): redevelopment was strictly controlled and almost entirely limited to rebuilding of bombed buildings and government offices. Also Royal Festival Hall, by Leslie Martin and R. Matthew (1951).

Second phase (1954–64): the boom years.
1954. Building licences removed. At once land prices jumped, plans began to be laid for dozens of development schemes.
1955. Woolworth House built in Marylebone Rd, by Richard Seifert.
1956. Plans published for New Zealand House, on site of Carlton Hotel at bottom of Haymarket. Clore buys row of elegant bomb-damaged houses in Park Lane, site of future Hilton Hotel, for £550,000. Row over London University's proposed demolition of Colcutt's Imperial Institute in Kensington (tower later saved).
1957. TUC headquarters in Great Russell St, built. Row over proposal to demolish part of Nash terraces in Regent's Park.
1958. Castrol House in Marylebone Rd, Bowater House in Knightsbridge introduced new type of glass-and-concrete office blocks. Row over destruction of Georgian terraces in Lincoln's Inn Fields by Royal College of Surgeons.
1959. 15-storey Thorn House in Upper St Martin's Lane, one of London's first new-style tower blocks (architects Basil Spence and Andrew Renton).
This was the year when the new property boom first broke into the headlines, as the number of deals in property shares jumped from 16,000 to 102,000, and Jack Cotton published plans for a 165-ft tower on the Monico site, Piccadilly Circus. Barbican scheme by Chamberlin, Powell and Bon finally agreed for vast bomb-levelled area of north-west City. Sir Leslie Martin's plan for long-term

New Zealand House, seen over the roof of the United Services Club

12

Shell Centre (1957–62), regarded in early sixties as chief symbol of new 'tower block' architecture

London University expansion into Bloomsbury squares. Mermaid Theatre conversion. Plans published for Stag Brewery development in Victoria, and Elephant and Castle.

1960. BBC-TV Centre at White City, and Saarinen's Grosvenor Square US Embassy opened. Cotton scheme for Piccadilly rejected after public inquiry. Row over plans to demolish Hardwick's Euston Station, especially Doric Arch.

1961. New Zealand House opened. 2nd Piccadilly scheme (by Holford) published.

1962. Londoners for the first time became aware of just what a transformation of London's skyline was taking place, with the rise or completion of the Shell Building on South Bank (351 ft), Vickers Tower on Millbank (387 ft), Hilton Hotel on Park Lane (328 ft) and Campden Tower on Notting Hill Gate. Londonderry House sold for £500,000. Euston Arch demolished.

1963. Huge Stag Place development completed, including

Euston Arch: demolition in 1962 was a cause célèbre

13

Goodbye London

London Wall

Portland House (334 ft). Carlton Tower completed in Sloane St. Coal Exchange in Lower Thames St pulled down. Property shares decline in value from their peak in 1962 (after an eightfold appreciation in four years), and Cotton-Clore-Flack association in City Centre, the world's largest property company, breaks up.

1964. St Paul's Precinct (Holford) completed, also *Economist* building in St James's. Barbican scheme beginning to appear, as tower blocks (owned by Hyams, Clore, Wates and others) rise along London Wall. Royal Garden Hotel (designed by Richard Seifert) overlooking Kensington Gardens. Bulldozers move in on 13 acres of Georgian and 19th-century terraces north of Euston Rd, for Joe Levy's Euston Centre scheme.

November. George Brown's ban on further office development.

Third phase: 1964–70: during this phase, following the Brown ban, the major office developments still rising were those for which contracts had been signed before 15th November 1964, e.g. the north side of Victoria St including City Hall.

1965. Centre Point completed at St Giles's Circus. GPO Tower (619 ft) opened in September. Sir Leslie Martin's scheme for Whitehall, including demolition of Foreign Office, Home Office and whole Richmond Terrace block published.

1966–70. Several more major office schemes came to completion during these years, such as the Euston Centre (1968) and Drapers Gardens (Hyams/Seifert 1967), but focus of redevelopment during this period changed to hotel building (Royal Lancaster and Cromwell Rd area), and institutional development: e.g. Kings College's destruction of two remaining 17th-century wooden-fronted houses in the Strand for extension, Basil Spence's Knightsbridge Barracks (1967–

70), the Swiss Centre (1967), and the Queen Elizabeth Hall, (GLC architects 1967). 1968 Covent Garden Plan published. 1969 Row over London University's plan to demolish Woburn Square.

Fourth phase: 1970 onwards. After return of Conservatives, office ban was lifted and everything got under way for huge new phase of redevelopment.

1972. Public inquiry into Covent Garden Comprehensive Development scheme. 4th Piccadilly scheme published. Row over Basil Spence/Harold Samuel scheme for Queen Anne's Mansions block. Growing public concern over whole question of massive redevelopment in London.

There is scarcely a single celebrated building in London which has not been threatened with demolition at one time or another. During the novelty mania of the sixties, schemes were mooted for the demolition of the Houses of Parliament, St Pancras station, Tower Bridge, the whole of the southern half of Whitehall including the Foreign Office, Whitehall Court and the Tate Gallery portico. This tide has receded a long way.

Far left, old Knightsbridge Barracks; left, as rebuilt by Sir Basil Spence

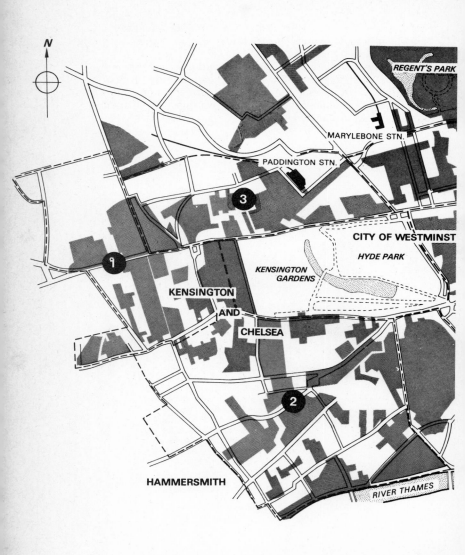

N

REGENT'S PARK

MARYLEBONE STN.

PADDINGTON STN.

3

CITY OF WESTMINST

HYDE PARK

KENSINGTON
GARDENS

9

KENSINGTON

AND

CHELSEA

2

HAMMERSMITH

RIVER THAMES

16

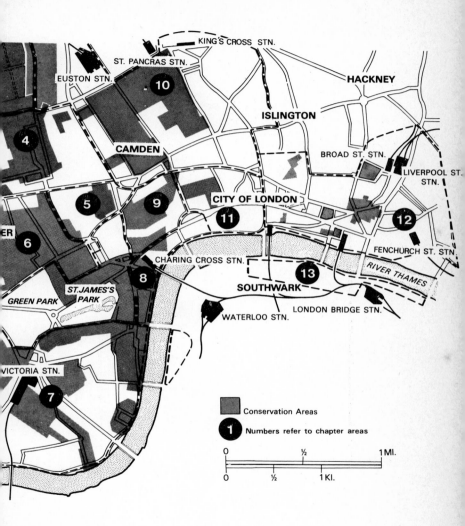

KING'S CROSS STN.

ST. PANCRAS STN.

EUSTON STN.

10

HACKNEY

ISLINGTON

4

CAMDEN

BROAD ST. STN.

LIVERPOOL ST. STN.

5   **9**   **CITY OF LONDON**

11   **12**

6   FENCHURCH ST. STN.

CHARING CROSS STN.

8   **13**   RIVER THAMES

SOUTHWARK

GREEN PARK   *ST. JAMES'S PARK*

WATERLOO STN.   LONDON BRIDGE STN.

VICTORIA STN.

7

Conservation Areas

1   Numbers refer to chapter areas

0   ½   1 MI.

0   ½   1 KI.

17

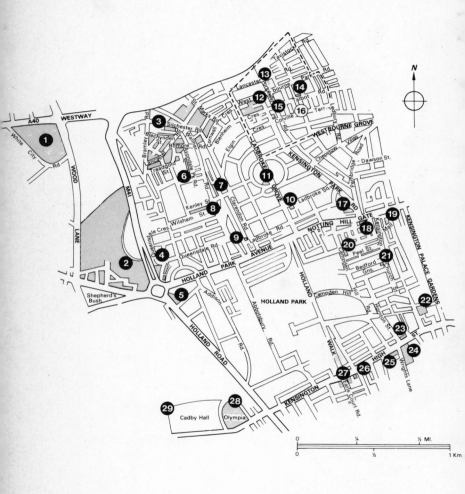

1. North-West Kensington

GLC housing, Norland area

Mainly a residential area of terraces and squares, built in the second half of the 19th century outwards from the villages of Kensington and Notting Hill. The chief changes likely in the area are several very large slum clearance and rehousing schemes, involving dozens of streets in the poorer areas to the north and west. Already new tower blocks have replaced 19th-century streets in the Norland area bordering the M41 and the Silchester area bordering Westway. Two other enormous schemes are under way for the Lancaster Rd West and Colville areas. Two famous sites scheduled for redevelopment just over the Hammersmith border are the White City stadium and the Olympia Exhibition Hall.

The north side of Notting Hill Gate was the scene of one of the big redevelopments of the early sixties (Campden Tower). Redevelopment has continued on both sides (e.g. recent Czech Centre by Sir R. Matthew) and remaining older buildings seem likely to follow (e.g. Gaumont cinema, group around Classic, and blocks east of Pembridge Rd).

The other main focus of change is Kensington High St, where likely major redevelopments will include the old Town Hall, Pontings, the Odeon, the underground station and the huge Rank Organisation scheme for the top of the Earls Court Rd, which has been argued over for several years.

1   White City Stadium. Built for London Olympics of 1908. Stock Conversion have outline planning permission for redevelopment of $16\frac{1}{2}$-acre site, including hotel, exhibition centre, warehousing and offices. The Greyhound Racing Association Property Trust plans new compact stadium across the road. All subject to decision on Channel Tunnel Terminal.

2   77-acre site north of Shepherds Bush Common. Original huge Taylor Woodrow scheme for redeveloping this entire site abandoned. After a 'public participation exercise' organised by Hammersmith in December 1972, large-scale piecemeal redevelopment seems likely for housing and other uses.

1

19

3a

3 Lancaster Rd West scheme. Involving redevelopment of 28 acres south of Railway, including: St Marks Rd (St Marks Church 1863), Cornwall Crescent, Talbot Grove, Lancaster Rd, Walmer Rd, Clarendon Rd, Silchester Rd, Blechynden Mews, Blechynden St, Bomore Rd, Fowell St, Grenfell, Tredgold St, Hurstway, Bramley Rd, Barandon St. These agreeably informal mid-19th-century streets have decayed over past ten years while future overshadowed by demolition proposals. The Silchester Estate tower blocks have already been built by the GLC.

P. Rehousing of 3,700 people, shopping precincts, schools, community services etc, at estimated cost of £20 million. **A.** Consortium of private architects, coordinated by Borough Architect Mr G. J. Woolnough. **D.** Kensington and Chelsea, ILEA and GPO.

3a, St Mark's Church; 3b and 3f, Silchester Rd; 3c, Lancaster Rd; 3d, Walmer Rd; 3e, Portland Rd; 3f, Silchester Rd

3d

3b
3c

3e
3f

North-West Kensington

4 Norland Rd, and Norland Gardens. This sadly-decayed little corner remains a memorial to planning confusion. Standing on the borough boundary between Kensington and Hammersmith, it would have provided an ideal intimately-scaled shopping centre and foil to the towering blocks of the GLC/Hammersmith housing estate to the north. As it is, the shops and houses stand mainly boarded up and empty, and the only plan seems to be Hammersmith's for an open space here by the year 2000.

4a-b, Norland Gardens (1833)

4a
4b

5b

5 188–202 Holland Rd, and Duke of Clarence public house. This site, along with 19–23 Upper Addison Gardens, has been subject to much speculation. Various applications for offices or hotel have been refused, owing to proximity of Shepherds Bush roundabout. Meanwhile site remains in limbo subject to decision on West Cross route.

5a, Upper Addison Gardens; 5b, Holland Rd

5b

5a

6

6 5–33 Avondale Park Rd. 19th-century cottages with front gardens. **P.** Flats, garaging. **A.** H. M. Greiller. **D.** Octavia Hill Housing Trust.

North-West Kensington

7   Hippodrome Mews. **P.** 32 houses. **A.** Michael Brown Associates. **D.** City Side Properties and Ariel Developments.

12, Kensington Park Rd

12   Site bounded by Westbourne Park Rd, Ladbroke Grove, Kensington Park Rd, and Blenheim Crescent (the Westbourne Park Rd Development Scheme). **P.** 120 flats. **A.** R. G. Hunter and Partners. **D.** Notting Hill Housing Trust in conjunction with Kensington and Chelsea Borough Council.

8

8   Wilsham St, and Kenley St. **P.** 19th-century streets to be redeveloped for housing. **A.** H. M. Greiller. **D.** Octavia Hill Housing Trust.

13, Portobello Rd

9   88–90 Ladbroke Rd. Typical example of the kind of infilling which has taken place in several parts of the Ladbroke Estate (despite Conservation area status). This elegant area is an example of some of the first Garden Planning and its leafy spaces form an integral part. **P.** Luxury flats. **A.** Colin White.

10   2–3 Ladbroke Square. After recent fire application has been made to redevelop in this previously untouched square. **A.** Lord Austin Smith.

11   63 Ladbroke Grove (Late-Victorian St Johns Vicarage) and 2 Lansdowne Crescent. **P.** New vicarage, church hall, flats. **A.** Denis Berry.

11

13   228–30 Portobello Rd and 1–10 Alba Place (since the 1800s the Portobello Rd has been the market centre for West Kensington). **P.** Large Supermarket. **A.** Edwin Hill and Partners. **D.** David Greig.

11, Ladbroke Grove

14

17a
17b

14 Talbot Rd, All Saints Church (1855).
P. Flats. **A.** Edward Stephan Associates.
15 Kensington Park Rd, Peniel Chapel.
P. Flats. **D.** E. A. S. Houfe.
16 The Colville Area. 60-acre area, laid
out around 1860s bounded by Westway,
Westbourne Grove, Ladbroke Grove,
Ledbury Rd, and St Luke's Rd, has been
the subject of extensive study by
Kensington and Chelsea Borough Council.
The Council's eventual aim is combination
of redevelopment and improvement of
existing properties, and provision of open
spaces and other amenities. Report to be
published in 1973.

17 Corner of Ladbroke Rd and
Pembridge Villas (including Prince Albert
public house). **P.** Office block and ballet
theatre. **D.** Mercury Theatre Trust for
Ballet Rambert.

16a

*16a, Colville Terrace; 16b, Colville
Square; 16c, Ledbury Rd; 17a, The
Prince Albert; 17b, Ladbroke Rd*

16c

16b

North-West Kensington

20   Lex Garage site, Campden Hill Rd (opposite old site of Water Tower) **P.** Offices, 96 flats. **A.** Stefan Zins Associates. **D.** Hills Structures and Foundations.

18

21

18   Notting Hill Gate, Gaumont Cinema. Formerly famous as Coronet Theatre, played in by Sarah Bernhardt and many others. **P.** Shops, offices, flats. **A.** Sidney Kaye, Eric Firmin and Partners. **D.** Rank Organisation.

21   1 Bedford Gardens (on corner of Kensington Church St). Kensington Society's attempt to get this prominent corner building listed failed. **P.** Antique shop, flats. **A.** Igal Yawetz Associates with M. Howard Radley.

19   2–8 Kensington Mall (Lucerne Chambers) and 2–16 Rabbit Row. **P.** Shops, offices, flats, car park. **A.** Ben Williams.

19a

22

22   Kensington Barracks, off Church St. NCP have temporarily leased site for car park, and Crown Estates have development plans for 'a diplomatic use'.

19a, Kensington Mall; 19b, Rabbit Row

19b

23

23 Town Hall, Kensington High St. Basil Spence's new £6½-million Town Hall behind public library will be completed by spring 1975, and 1878 Town Hall will then be sold for redevelopment.

25

25 Iverna Court and properties fronting Kensington High St. Recently bought by Commerical Union for £8 million. New owners have no plans for redevelopment at present.

24 121–7 Kensington High St (Pontings and underground station), and east side of Wrights Lane. **P.** Offices, 150 flats, shopping precinct. **D.** Star (Great Britain).

24a

26 229–31 Kensington High St. **P.** Store with offices above. **A.** Morrison, Rose.

24a, Pontings; 24b, underground station

24b

North-West Kensington

28 Olympia. Exhibition Hall with cast-iron canopy 1884, and 1930 extensions. With plans for new national exhibition hall at Northolt and Surrey Docks (see also Earls Court), redevelopment by owners (35% Associated Newspapers, 18% Sterling Guarantee) seems likely.

28

27 217–25 Kensington High St (including Odeon cinema), and 1–23 and 4–30 Earls Court Rd. This major site has a complicated planning history. Various schemes including a hotel have been turned down by the Council. The most recent application was for 100–150,000 sq ft offices, shops and flats, including a 90-ft block bridging the Earls Court Rd. Eventual development will set the tone for the new High St. **A.** Sidney Kaye. **D.** Rank Organisation.

29 Cadby Hall. J. Lyons wish to redevelop this 10-acre site, although plans for 1000-bedroom hotel, 338 flats and 272,750 sq ft offices were turned down by Hammersmith.

Late entry (not on map)

30 1–7 Kensington Church St, 20–21 Kensington Church Walk. Although recently advertised as suitable for redevelopment, Council are unlikely to give permission.

7b

27a, Odeon cinema; 27b, Earls Court Rd

2. South Kensington and Chelsea

Penta Hotel (Seifert)

In recent years this mainly residential area has been under considerable pressure from new hotel and office schemes. 37 hotels and 3 million sq ft office development were current in late 1972, and the Borough has sought Parliamentary powers to limit the problem. Nowhere is being more rapidly transformed than the Cromwell Rd, where huge tower block hotels, such as the Seifert-designed 270-ft high London Penta ('London's biggest post-war hotel') are rising over what remains of the porticoed 19th-century terraces. Even the President of the London Tourist Board, Lord Mancroft, has warned of the dangers of this area becoming a 'Costa Cromwellia'. The Kings Rd has already lost much of its traditional character in the boom years since 1964, although a number of large new schemes are brewing in the area, led by that on the Pheasantry block, and several sites seem likely candidates for redevelopment in the next few years (including the large British Road Services depot standing behind the south side frontage), but planning proposals had not been put forward by the end of 1972.

Huge changes are likely along the park frontage between Kensington High St and Knightsbridge, already dominated by Seifert's Royal Garden Hotel and Spence's Knightsbridge Barracks.

Some years ago, Capital and Counties produced an elaborate scheme for the junction of Knightsbridge, Brompton Rd and Sloane St — a new 'gateway to London' — but this has been abandoned, and development of the area is piecemeal. Capital and Counties have already begun this, e.g. their cylindrical Park Tower Hotel designed by Richard Seifert, on the old Woollands site.

28

South Kensington and Chelsea

1   Warwick Rd, Warwick Gardens and
Pembroke Rd. **P.** Central Works Depot on
south corner of Warwick and Pembroke
Rd. Housing on opposite corner. **A.** Arup
Associates. **D.** Royal Borough of
Kensington and Chelsea.
2   Wrights Lane, Church of Christ
Scientist. **P.** Offices, flats, car park,
church.
3   Site off Wrights Lane behind Pontings.
P. London Tara Hotel, shops, car park
(under construction). **D.** Aer Lingus.

5

4, De Vere Mews

5   Thorney Court, on corner of Palace
Gate and 55 Hyde Park Gate. This 1907
mansion block was pulled down before
planning permission for redevelopment
had been received. Plan for hotel was
refused, and owners have now been
granted permission for 56 flats. The old
Thorney Court contained 54 flats.
A. Louis de Soissons Partnership.

6   5–8 Hyde Park Gate. **P.** Flats,
garaging. **A.** Triad.

4   De Vere Mews, Canning Place Mews,
De Vere Gardens and Canning Place. The
De Vere Mews stables, still used, are one
of the last in central London (another off
Regents Park is also threatened). **P.**
Conversion into luxury maisonettes.
A. Triad. **D.** Barlow Cannon Estates.

6

29

South Kensington & Chelsea

7 197–9 Queens Gate and Park frontage to Jay Mews. Likely to be demolished by Royal College of Art for new extension. Original plans involved redevelopment of whole block including 196 (one of three houses in Queens Gate by Norman Shaw) but, after outcry, these have now been modified to exclude the
7a Shaw building.

9 1–7 Rutland Gate. Demolition contractors' boards up although plans by Richard Seifert for a residential centre for High Commissions are in abeyance. 9
10 243–5 Knightsbridge, and South Lodge, a large detached house, with cottage and stable yard. **P.** Terrace houses, flats, offices in slab block. **A.** Chapman Taylor. **D.** Trafalgar House.
11 32–44 Hans Crescent (Demolished 1972). **P.** Offices, shops. **A.** D. A. Mailer. **D.** Capital and Counties.

10a, South Lodge; 10b, Knightsbridge

7b

7a, Queens Gate; 7b, Park Frontage

10a

10b

8 191–4 Queens Gate. Threatened by Imperial College's rebuilding programme (which had already involved the destruction, in highly controversial circumstances, of 177–80, the last by Norman Shaw). Perhaps moved by notoriety they received from demolition of 180 in 1970, College has now announced that it has 'no more plans for rebuilding in Central London'.

14

14 South Kensington underground station. Plans for 14 storey hotel extending down Pelham Place were given outline consent some years ago against the advice of the Royal Fine Arts Commission, but appear to be in abeyance. Demolition down Pelham Place has already taken place in connection with London Transport's reconstruction of station.

12

12 12–30 Hans Rd. 12, 14, 16 by Voysey, with fine interiors. Three different proposals have been made for conversion of interiors to office and/or hotel use, the last subject to a public inquiry in March 1972. **P.** Conversion to offices and flats. **A.** Dennis Lennon and Partners.

13

15

13 171–5 Brompton Rd (formerly El Cubano). **P.** Shops, offices, flats. **A.** Igal Yawetz.

15 1–3 Harrington Gardens. **P.** Offices, flats, car park. **A.** J. Elia Shaul.
16 Site bounded by 4–18 Harrington Gardens, 1–13 Courtfield Rd, 16–30 Ashburn Place. **P.** Gloucester Hotel, nearing completion. **A.** Sidney Kaye.
D. Rank Organisation for Sheraton Hotels.

17a
17b

18a
18b

17 Site bounded by Cromwell Rd, Gloucester Rd, Courtfield Rd, and Ashburn Place. There have been various plans for this 3-acre site, which in 1972 was sold by Swordheath Properties to Eastern and General Holdings for £5·9 million.
P. Offices, shops, flats (430,000 sq ft).
A. Gollins Melvin Ward.

17a Ashburn Place; 17b, Ashburn Mews; 17c, Gloucester Rd

18 Site bounded by Cromwell Rd, Gloucester Rd, Southwell Gardens and Grenville Place (St Stephens Precinct), excluding St Stephens Church. Large area owned by Lamington Properties who are fighting a losing battle against damage caused by traffic vibration, and are considering redevelopment. Original application included 9-storey block.

18a, Grenville Place; 18b, Gloucester Rd

17c

South Kensington and Chelsea

19 Emperors Gate, south-west side. Flats here demolished by Trust Houses Forte, who hoped to build £6 million tower-block hotel. Because of large number of other hotel projects in the area, THF applied to build a car park instead. This proposal was refused. The site at present lies dormant and local residents are pressing for flats.

'developers' blight'. In 1970 offers were made by estate agents to persuade 100 residents and shopkeepers to get out within two months, on the grounds that redevelopment was imminent. The large modern block of flats on Cromwell Rd was demolished, and the rest of the property left to decay. Two years later nothing had happened. In 1972 Edger Investments bought the site from Legal and Merchant Securities, and applied for permission to build a 180-ft tower hotel and a 120-ft tower of offices and flats (by Stone, Toms and Partners). The Council, however, made it clear that they disliked the scheme on the grounds of 'overdevelopment', and that there can be no question of replacing demolished flats by offices.

20

20 174–6 Cromwell Rd. **P.** Hotel. **A.** Karnel Consultants.
21 180–6 Cromwell Rd. Site boarded off in 1972 prior to demolition, but no planning application yet made.

22 Site bounded by Cromwell Rd, Earls Court Rd, Redfield Lane including Redfield Mews. A classic tale of

22, Redfield Lane

23

23 150–8 Earls Court Rd. **P.** Shops, offices, flats. **D.** Burt Hamilton Investments.
24 Earls Court Exhibition Hall (see also Olympia). Following plans for new national exhibition centre, this 18 acre site was bought for £5·5 million in March 1972 by a consortium made up of Sterling Guarantee and Town and City. Plans for comprehensive redevelopment costing over £50 million.

24

25

29

25 223–7 Earls Court Rd (YWCA).
P. 10-storey hostel. **A.** J. A. Starling.
D. YWCA.
26 2a Bina Gardens and 1, 2, 2a Dove
Mews. **P.** Offices, flats. **A.** Norman
Ashley Green.
27 123–33 Old Brompton Rd. **P.**
Offices, flats. **Ap.** A. Knight.
28 Cranley Gardens, St Peter's Church.
Threatened by financial difficulties.
29 75–97 Elm Park Gardens. **P.** 60
flats, garaging. **D.** Kensington and
Chelsea Borough Council.
30 158–76 Fulham Rd and Canvey
Place, including pub and Regency
houses. **P.** Shops, offices. **A.** Turner
Lansdowne Holt. **D.** Bovis.
31 186–8 Fulham Rd. **P.** Offices, shops.
A. J. P. Caneparo and Associates.

30a, Canvey Place; 30b, Fulham Rd

30a
30b

28

S. Kensington & Chelsea

34   Site between Edith Grove, Kings Rd and Cheyne Walk (World's End Redevelopment Scheme). Much of site under construction. **P.** Housing, offices, shops, church. **A.** Eric Lyons Cadbury Brown and Partnership and Borough Architect. **D.** Kensington and Chelsea.

35   279 Kings Rd (Essoldo cinema). **P.** Conversion into 4 cinemas.

36   32–7 Cheyne Walk, 58–69 Oakley St (including Pier Hotel and billiard table works). This well-known group was demolished amid considerable controversy in the mid-sixties, supposedly to make way for a tower block. Under a new scheme the site is to be filled with 129 flats, which is hardly more than the original content. **A.** R. R. Martin. **D.** Cadogan Estates.

37   33 Tite St (Studios by Godwin). Although the building is not to share the fate of Whistler's White House at 35, also by Godwin (destroyed in 1964), it may be converted into 9 flats. **D.** Metropolitan and Westcliff Investments.

32

38

32   Sandford Manor, Sandford Road, S. of Kings Road. Decayed 17th-century manor house, once the home of Nell Gwynn. Owners, Romulus, hope to develop surrounding sites with shops, offices, warehousing and flats. It seems unlikely the Manor will survive.

33   536 Kings Rd. **P.** Offices, flats. **A.** Sir John Burnet Tait and Partners.

34, Kings Rd

38   1–5 Christchurch St. **P.** Residential and garaging. **A.** J. A. Paterson Morgan.

39   Kings Road, Odeon cinema. **P.** Conversion into double cinema. **D.** Rank.

40   194–8 Kings Rd. **P.** Supermarket. **A.** Oscar Garry and Partners.

44, John Lewis warehouse

44 Site bounded by Sloane Avenue, Ixworth Place and Draycott Avenue. (John Lewis warehouse and Marlborough School). **P.** Supermarket, offices, flats, warehousing, school. **A.** Tripe and Wakeham and Partnership.

41, Jubilee Place

41 152–68 Kings Rd, 3–5 and 8–24 Jubilee Place, 1–4 Joubert Studios, 6 Burnsall St (the Pheasantry site). Various schemes have been put forward. The latest, which seems likely to go through, is for offices, flats and car-parking. The Pheasantry facade will be retained, although large studios behind and interesting turreted stone tower-house in Jubilee Place will go. **A.** Michael Lyell Associates. **D.** Charles Cyzer.

42

45

42 150 Kings Rd (Classic cinema). Sold by Laurie Marsh, Dec. 1972, for redevelopment.
43 Draycott Avenue, Guinness Trust Housing Estate. **P.** 10-storey flats. **D.** Guiness Trust.

45 Corner of Fulham Rd and Sloane Avenue (Michelin Building). Well-known art nouveau showpiece. Michelin hope to redevelop this site into 93,000 sq ft offices. Tiled facades at northern end will probably be retained.
46 36a Halsey St. **P.** 3 new houses. **A.** Michael Brown Associates.

49   Site bounded by 54–60 Sloane St, Hans St and Pavilion Rd. Presently an NCP car park and likely to remain vacant for some time since plans for new Danish Embassy, which have outline permission, are in abeyance.

50

47   Sloane St, Holy Trinity Church (J. D. Sedding 1888–9). The Cadogan Estate have been interested in redevelopment with flats and a smaller church, but no proposals have been put forward.

Late entry (not on map)

50   140–2 Gloucester Rd and Grenville Mews (Bailey's Hotel). **P.** Offices, shops, flats. **A.** Michael R. Blampied and Partners. **D.** Marcrest Properties.

48   Sloane Square

48   Site bounded by Sloane Square, Kings Rd, Cheltenham Terrace, Lower Sloane St and Turks Row (including offices and shops fronting onto Sloane Square and Duke of York's Headquarters behind). Redevelopment is in the air for parts of site, which is owned by Cadogan Estate.

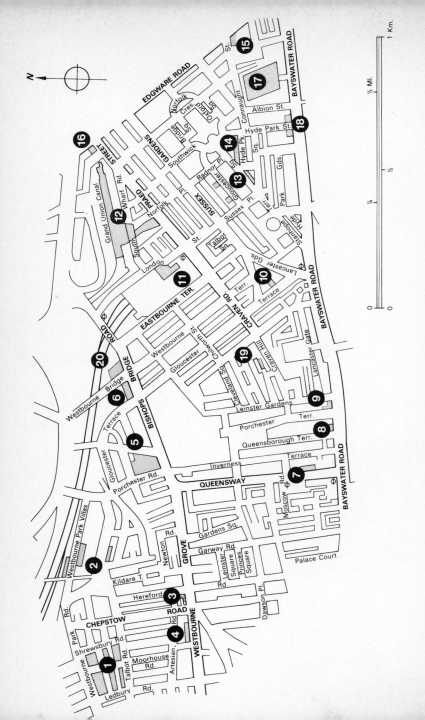

3. Paddington and Bayswater

New Queensway

This area stretches from decayed Victorian middle-class terraces in the north west, through the more elegant stucco of Bayswater to the towering new blocks of luxury flats behind and along the Edgware Rd.

Recent redevelopment has been considerable. Among the major developments of the late fifties and early sixties were the new office blocks along Eastbourne Terrace west of Paddington Station (the two largest being those by Sir Max Rayne in conjunction with the Church Commissioners, and Telstar House at the north end, built for Harry Hyams by Richard Seifert). On either side of Edgware Rd, by the Westway flyover, stand two more Seifert blocks, Foster Wheeler House in front of Marks and Spencer, and the new Metropole Hotel. Further down are the Wates' tower-block flats on the Church's Paddington Estate (1967–70), and in the late sixties Bayswater saw a number of new hotels, including the Royal Lancaster overlooking the Park (1967).

Westminster Council and the GLC have large slum clearance and rehabilitation schemes in the north west (bordering Kensington's huge Colville scheme at Ledbury Rd). Westway has created 'motorway blight' along its length, and few older buildings are likely to survive (as between North Wharf Rd, and Harrow Rd). Other likely centres of development in the coming years are Westbourne Grove, Queensway and some of the remaining older parts of the Church Commissioners' Hyde Park Estate — although the report prepared for the Commissioners by Leslie Lane in 1972 suggests that more properties on the estate will be retained than previously seemed likely, including Sussex Gardens.

1a

1b

4a

4b

1a, St Stephen's Gardens; 1b, Talbot Rd

4a, Needham Rd; 4b, Westbourne Grove

1 Site bounded by Westbourne Park Rd, Ledbury Rd, Talbot Rd, and Shrewsbury Rd (St Stephen's Redevelopment Scheme). These four blocks, including mews in between, are to be redeveloped by Westminster City Council as part of a large housing scheme. An extension of Great Western road will run across the site into Chepstow Rd.
2 78–84 and 87–101 Westbourne Park Villas. Mostly boarded-up preparatory to demolition, but no application as yet.

4 142–52 Westbourne Grove, 2–8 Needham Rd. The Utopian Voluntary Housing Society obtained planning permission for 48 flats on this site, but failed to buy the property.
5 Site bounded by Porchester Rd, Bishops Bridge Rd, Porchester Terrace and Porchester Square (up to Porchester Square Mews). Large development in conservation area, already under construction. In September 1972 the Secretary of State for the Environment ordered an inquiry into how the developers had obtained the concession to develop the site from its owners, Westminster City Council. In November 1972 the inquiry was postponed. **P.** Offices, flats, shops, library, car parking. **A.** Farrell Grimshaw Partnership. **D.** Elystan Developments, a subsidiary of Samuel Properties.

3

3 98–104 Westbourne Grove, and 6 Botts Mews. **P.** Shops, offices, flats. **D.** J. A. Garland.

Paddington and Bayswater

6

8

8 117–18 Bayswater Rd. Have been allowed to decay, although as yet there is no planning application for redevelopment.

6 Holy Trinity, Bishops Bridge Rd (Thomas Cundy 1843). The spire was taken down in 1972, and the rest of the church will soon follow. Demolition was made virtually inevitable by stone decay, accelerated by diesel fumes from Paddington Station. British Rail refused to accept partial responsibility.

9, Bayswater Rd

7

9 100–3 Bayswater Rd, 1, 1a, 3 and 5 Porchester Terrace. This site has had a long and interesting history. 100 and 101, listed, are two-storey Regency Cottages, the last in Bayswater Rd. In Porchester Terrace are three large detached early-Victorian houses, two of them listed. Various attempts have been made to redevelop, the latest by Mesco Properties in January 1971, who went bankrupt when their hotel scheme was refused. The property was sold in October 1972 to Leeds and London Securities. An appeal against refusal to allow redevelopment was heard in December 1972.

7 28–44 Queensway. This block, one of the few remaining original stretches of the street, is being bought up by a developer through estate agents Michael Koopman and Partners, for eventual redevelopment.

10 *10*   **13** *13*

10 Westbourne Terrace, St Stephen's Church. Future uncertain.
11 Paddington Station. Most of the station, including Brunel's cast-iron canopy, is a Grade One listed building. Reconstruction has been proposed at the south-eastern end which will affect the ends of the great spans of Brunel's train shed.
12 Grand Union Canal, Paddington Basin. St Mary's Hospital have plans for £23-million extension over part of 100,000 sq ft open water. After strong opposition, a public inquiry was held in the summer of 1972. Westminster supported the plans, but the GLC are concerned at the loss of a valuable potential 'leisure area'. Whatever happens, extensive redevelopment seems likely in whole area between South Wharf Rd and Westway. Freeholders, Grand Junction Co, recently bought by Amalgamated Investments.

13 Gloucester Square, south side (George Leadwell Taylor). The Church Commissioners in their Hyde Park Estate Report envisage redevelopment of this 1830 stucco block and two remaining fragments of original square on the north side, between 1975 and 1980.

12   *14*

14 Hyde Park Square, north side (George Leadwell Taylor, post-1837). The Church Commissioners envisage redevelopment in 1980s.
15 26 Edgware Rd, National Westminster Bank. This Italianate stucco building is listed Grade II. Leslie Lane, in their Hyde Park Estate Report, recommend redevelopment.

15

19 6, 7, 8 Craven Hill Mews. **P.** 6
houses. **A.** Inskip and Wilczynski.
20 Site on corner of Bishops Bridge Rd
and Westbourne Terrace, formerly part of
stucco Westbourne Terrace. Presently
leased by NCP from Westminster, who
will redevelop for housing.

Late entries (not on map)
21 50–8 Westbourne Grove (one of
last surviving stretches of original street).
P. Offices, shops. **A.** Grinling and Crisp.

16, Praed St

16 Site bounded by Edgware Rd, Praed
St and Irongate Wharf Rd (Harbet Rd),
including Duke of Wellington public
house. This site, already half-cleared, is
south of Richard Seifert's new 550-
bedroom Metropole Hotel for AVP
Industries on land belonging to Inland
Waterways. Seifert-AVP combination may
extend development south with shopping
precinct and flats when collection of
leases is complete.
17 Burial ground off Albion St (formerly
belonging to St George's Hanover
Square). One of London 'secret gardens'.
Bought in the late sixties by the Utopian
Voluntary Housing Society, for a large
housing development (architects: Design
5) which was almost complete in 1972.

22

22 18–24 Westbourne Grove (Fred.
Lawrence). **P.** Offices, shops, flats.
A. Michael Lyall Associates.
23 Island site bounded by Queensway,
Redan Place and Porchester Gdns.
William Whiteley's London's first
department store. **P.** hotel, offices, shops,
car park. **A.** Sidney Kaye. **D.** United
Drapery Stores.
24 West corner Bayswater Rd, Elms
Mews (including Swan public house).
Park Plaza Hotel have applied for
extension on this site.

18 Hyde Park St. Two large stucco
blocks on corner with Bayswater Rd
scheduled for redevelopment by Church
Commissioners in 1980s.

18

43

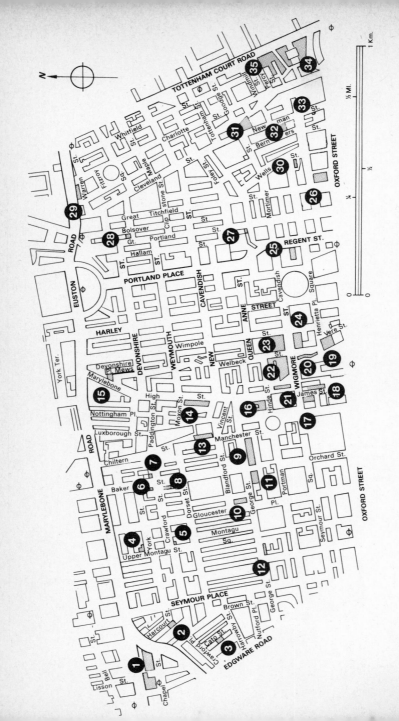

New bank, Oxford St (Seifert)

4. North of Oxford Street

This area may be roughly divided into five districts. On the west stand the mainly residential squares, mews and little streets of Georgian houses and shops on each side of Baker St. The centre is dominated by the tall, austere houses of the medical profession, round Harley St and Wimpole St. To the south lie the busy shopping thoroughfares of Wigmore St and Oxford St. To the east of upper Regent St these give way to the rather gloomy redbrick corridors of Great Portland St and the rag trade, around Berners St. And bordering Tottenham Court Rd, is the more attractive area known as north Soho, centred on the restaurants and old artists' haunts of Charlotte and Percy St.

In the west, the recent developments by Max Rayne's London Merchant Securities on the Portman Estate have cut a swathe through the George St area, including listed buildings. Several schemes and proposals are still outstanding but opposition is likely to increase.

There have been a number of criticised developments on the Howard de Walden Estate round Harley St (now a Conservation Area), but one big scheme here was halted on the initiative of the Westminster planning officer. Further south, the march of new office blocks continues east down Wigmore St, although one or two large proposals now seem to be running into difficulties, with Westminster insisting on higher design standards. Several remaining old blocks along the north side of Oxford St seem likely to follow the old Marshall and Snelgrove store, (as Waring and Gillow to the east, shortly to be replaced by a large Seifert-designed block).

Considerable piecemeal development is taking place all through the east of the area, dominated in the north by the characterless boxes round the GPO Tower (Max Rayne's redevelopment of the old Cartwright Estate). Over the Camden boundary, the huge EMI scheme south of Percy St has run into difficulties, although it seems likely that the increasingly shabby area round the south-west end of the Tottenham Court Rd will see major changes before long.

1a, underground station; 1b, Chapel St

3   34–5 Cato St. **P.** Flats. **A.** Joseph Mendelson.

1   1–20 Chapel St (including Edgware Rd South underground station). **P.** Shops, flats, offices, booking hall. **A.** Richard Seifert. Seifert's third tower block development in a row at the Edgware Rd/ Westway crossing.

4   52–4 York St and 42–54 Upper Montague St. Showing signs of 'developer's blight'. Westminster served building preservation notices on five of the houses in December 1972. Owned by Portman Estate.

5   103–5 Crawford St. **P.** Offices, flats, shop. **Ap.** Karl Fisher.

2   26–8 Harcourt St. **P.** Flats, offices and Listed Building Demolition Consent. **A.** Dinerman Davison Associates.

6, Baker St/Crawford St

6 91–3 Baker St, 1–7 Crawford St, 7 Durweston Mews. **P.** Offices, shops, flats. **A.** C. H. Elsom Pack.

8, Baker St/Crawford St

8 87–9 Baker St, 127–30 Crawford St. **P.** Shops, offices, flats. **A.** Fewster and Partners.

7 96–8 Baker St (Classic cinema). **P.** Offices, flats, cinema. **A.** Doughton Hurst. Laurie Marsh Group has recently bought up Classic cinema chain with view to greater exploitation of sites.

7

9, George St

9 Site bounded by Baker St, George St, Manchester St and Robert Adam St. This large site, which included Georgian terrace of shops and houses in George St and St Paul's Church, is to serve temporarily as NCP car park. **P.** Shops, offices, flats. **A.** C. H. Elsom Pack. **D.** London Merchant Securities.

10, Gloucester Place

10 Site bounded by 24–40 Gloucester Place, Carton St, Blandford and George St. This continues existing development between Baker St and Carton St. Houses in Gloucester Place were listed but allowed to decay. Council has insisted on rebuilding behind replica facades in order to preserve homogeneity of street. **P.** Flats, offices. **A.** C. H. Elsom Pack, **D.** London Merchant Securities.
11 5–17 Baker St, 51–65 George St, 26–34 Portman Close. **P.** Offices, shops, flats. **A.** Sir John Burnet Tait and Partners. **D.** Tamlyn Properties.
12 117–25 George St, 1–3 Montague Mews (listed 18th-century houses). **P.** Offices, garages. **A.** C. H. Elsom Pack. **D.** London Merchant Securities.

11, George St

12, George St

13   20–7 Manchester St (listed Georgian terrace houses). **P.** Offices, flats. **A.** C. H. Elsom Pack. **D.** London Merchant Securities. Refused Jan. 1973.

14   Site bounded by Marylebone High St, Vincent St, Moxon St, Cramer St. T. P. Bennett and Son's application for redevelopment for shops, flats, offices and car park has so far been refused, although houses in Moxon St are already vacated ready for demolition.

15   55–7 Marylebone High St, 28–30 Beaumont St and 21–4 Devonshire Place Mews. **P.** Shops, flats. **D.** Howard de Walden Estates.

16a, Hinde St; 16b, Jacobs Well Mews   *16b*

16   11–14 Hinde St (Hinde House), 16–18 Thayer St and south end of Jacobs Well Mews. **P.** Offices, shops, flats. **A.** E. S. Boyer and Partners. (Refused Feb. 1973.)

17   79–93 Wigmore St, James St, 1–2 Picton Place. **P.** Shops, offices. **D.** Stock Conversion.

14, Moxon St

18

18   1–5 Barrett St, St Christopher's Place (including Antique Supermarket). **P.** Offices, flats (with retention of shops in St Christopher's Place). **D.** Greengarden Investments.

19 Site bounded by Marylebone Lane, Henrietta Place and Vere St. Marshall and Snelgrove completing redevelopment of their Oxford St store.

20 Site bounded by Wigmore St, Welbeck St and 38–46 Marylebone Lane. **P.** Offices, shops, flats, garage. **A.** Richard Seifert.

21 78–82 Wigmore St, 2–14 Mandeville Place (Mandeville Hotel). **P.** Hotel. **D.** Grand Metropolitan Hotels. Refused so far.

22 Site bounded by Wigmore St, Marylebone Lane, Bentinck St and Welbeck St (including John Bell and Croydon). **P.** £16-million scheme for offices, shops, hotel (retaining frontages to Welbeck and Bentinck St). **D.** Howard de Walden Estates.

20

23

23 Site bounded by Wigmore St, Welbeck St, Welbeck Way, Wimpole St (excluding Wigmore Hall and 42–8 Wigmore St). **P.** Shops, offices, flats. **D.** Prudential Assurance. Refused so far on grounds that designs fail to preserve architectural variety of existing buildings.

24 25–37 Wigmore St, 1–3 Welbeck St, 90–5 Wimpole St (Debenham and Freebody's, 1907). **P.** Offices, shops, bank. **A.** Richard Seifert.

25 Regent Street Polytechnic. Redevelopment proposals for 309 Regent St and Balderton St in the air.

22a
22b

22a, Wigmore St; 22b, Marylebone Lane

28

26 164–82 Oxford St, Waring and Gillow ('most elegant building in Oxford St'). **P.** Store, 198,000 sq ft offices in 9-storey block. **A.** Richard Seifert. **D.** Amalgamated Investments.
27 79–83 Great Portland St, 5–11 Riding House St. **P.** Offices, shops, flats. **A.** Sir John Burnet Tait and Partners.
28 73–4 Bolsover St and Church Hall in Great Portland St. **P.** Offices, shops. **A.** Chapman Taylor. This whole block up to Euston Rd is being developed piecemeal.
29 Site bounded by Euston Rd, Warren St, Conway St. **P.** 50,000 sq ft warehousing. **D.** Pirelli.

24

26
27

30 72–4 Wells St, 8 Marylebone Passage. **P.** Offices, flats. **A.** Trehearne and Norman Preston and Partners.

30

31, Goodge St

31 40–8 Newman St, 61 Goodge St.
P. Offices, shops, flats. Refused so far.
A. Newman Levinson.

32 63–4 Newman St, 16–17 Berners
Mews. **P.** Offices, shops. **A.** Hallam
Begby.

33, Newman St

33 87–91 Newman St, 5–7 Berners
Place (some of last remaining Georgian
houses in original Newman St). **P.**
Offices, workrooms, flats. **A.** Chapman
Taylor.

34

34 One-storey shops and restaurants
along Tottenham Court Rd (south west),
on site bounded by Hanway St, Hanway
Place and Tudor Place. Camden Council
have asked owners for redevelopment as
soon as possible.

N. of Oxford St

Late entries (not on map)

36 21 Little Portland St. Bovingdon and Fowler McBride have applied for permission to redevelop to provide showrooms, offices, etc.

37

35a, Tottenham Court Rd; 35b, Percy St

35 14–19 Percy St (18th-century), 18–38 Tottenham Court Rd, 1–13 Stephen St (18th-century) 19–25 Rathbone Place and properties in Gressey St, Stephens Mews, Gressy Buildings and Tudor Place. The site of a large EMI redevelopment scheme for shops, studios, offices, cinemas, flats and other uses, which was turned down by Camden Council on 15th October 1971. Council awaiting new proposals. **A.** Sidney Kaye.

37 79–84 Tottenham Court Rd. Victorian shops, Owners, Stock Conversion, seeking ODP for large office development.
38 64–6 Gt Portland St, 17 Little Titchfield St. **P.** Offices, shops. **A.** Fitzroy Robinson.
39 55–73 Gt Portland St. **P.** Offices, shops. **A.** Sir J. Burnet Tait. **D.** Laing.
40 56–62 Charlotte St (Scala Theatre site). **P.** Offices, shops, flats in 2 towers. **A.** Sidney Belfer. **D.** Consolidated Prop. Investments.

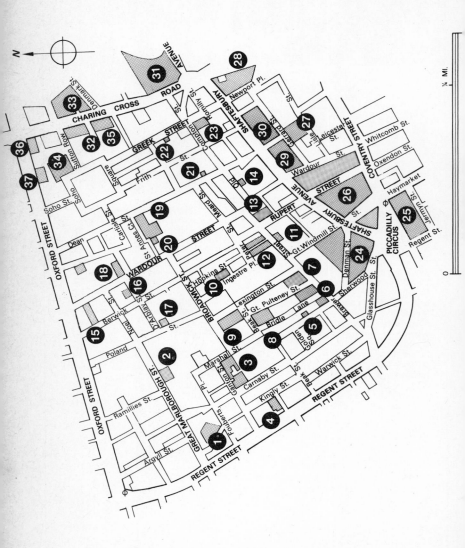

5. Soho

Ganton St

London's most central 'village', with its narrow streets and alleys, cosmopolitan restaurants and food shops, small businesses, street markets and 18th-century houses, has been comparatively unaffected by recent development. Only Wingate House (Columbia cinema) on Shaftesbury Avenue (1959), the 170-ft tower of council flats in Berwick St (1961) and recent blocks around Marshall St stand out. The main changes in Soho's character in the past decade have been the arrival of the strip clubs and 'Books and Mags', the boutiques of Carnaby St, and the 'Chinatown' which has established itself along the length of Gerrard St.

Now there are a mass of proposals, most of them comparatively small-scale, but dominated by the future of Piccadilly Circus. This is where the greatest changes will take place, even though the massive complex of blocks and towers originally proposed is not now likely (see separate entries). Another area of major change will be the west side of Charing Cross Rd, with Westminster planning a loop road behind new office blocks at the top, near the corner of Oxford St. The south side of Shaftesbury Avenue too may soon be a continuous strip of modern development, from Piccadilly Circus to High Holborn.

Other prominent sites affected are the Kettner's and Wheeler's restaurant block in Compton St and the fine Novello House in Wardour St, already boarded up, although this is in fact to be retained. The most conspicuous threat to Soho's traditional character must be the series of redevelopments planned by the Sutton Estate, on its properties north from Brewer St. Here are 18th-century houses and shops, Victorian pubs and a mass of small businesses, many long-established and well-known. The 'Button Shop' on Brewer St has already gone, and many others are threatened (not least the specialist food shops Lina's and Randall's, included in a nearby Westminster slum clearance scheme).

Soho

1 Behind Liberty's into Foubert's Place. **P.** 97,500 sq ft extension to store. **A.** William Holford. **D.** Liberty's. Consent given in 1969 but not yet acted on.

6a, Brewer St

2 51–3 Great Marlborough St (Victorian/ Edwardian shops, houses). **P.** Offices, shops. **A.** Richard Seifert. **D.** Taylor Investments. Turned down by Westminster, although buildings already half-demolished.

3 Site bounded by 10–20 Carnaby St, Ganton St, Marshall St. **P.** 62,500 sq ft offices in 12-storey tower, 23,500 sq ft shops, 36 flats, car park. **A.** D. Marriot, Worby and Robinson. **D.** LEB with Clarebrooke Holdings. Present proposal turned down Jan, 1973. Clarebrooke were given consent in October 1972 for 22,500 sq ft showrooms and flats on Marshall House site, with link across Marshall St.

4 St Thomas's Church, Kingly St. (1702). **P.** Offices, shops, flats, car park. **A.** Scott, Brownrigg and Turner.

5 8 Golden Square. **P.** Offices. **A.** Richard Seifert.

6 46–52 Brewer St, 35–43 Great Pulteney St, 1–5 Bridle Lane (including old family businesses and 18th-century houses). **P.** Offices, shops, flats (with rehabilitation of listed buildings). **A.** Cubitt Nichols. **O.** Sutton Settled Estates.

7 36–44 Brewer St, 1–5 Lexington St, 1 Gt Pulteney St (including old 'Button Shop'). Demolished 1972. **P.** Offices, shops. **A.** Cubitt Nicholas. **D.** Wates for Sutton Settled Estates.

6b, Great Pulteney St

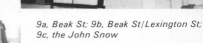

8a, Great Pulteney St; 8b, Sun and 13 Cantons

8 42–8 Beak St, 21–3 Gt Pulteney St, 17 Bridle Lane (including listed 18th-century buildings and Sun and 13 Cantons public house). **P.** Redevelopment for offices, shops, light industry. **A.** Cubitt Nichols. **O.** Sutton Settled Estates.

9a, Beak St; 9b, Beak St/Lexington St; 9c, the John Snow

9 73–9 Beak St, 41–53 Lexington St, 39–43 Broadwick St, (including old-established small businesses, gunsmiths, locksmiths, art gallery, 18th-century houses and John Snow public house). **A.** Cubitt Nichols. **O.** Sutton Settled Estates.

Soho

10 Site bounded by Ingestre Place and Hopkins St. Westminster City Council is erecting tower block including offices and 52 flats.
11 Brewer St, St James's Residences (low rent flats). Owned by Land Securities whose plans for redevelopment are unlikely to include much low-cost housing.

13

12a
12b

13 Corner of Rupert St and Brewer St. To be redeveloped for various uses, including a cinema, by G. and W. Walker, although details not yet public.
14 35 Old Compton St. **P.** Offices, flats. **A.** Newman, Levinson.

15, Berwick St

12a, Green's Court; 12b, Brewer St

12 14–22 Brewer St, 24–6 Peter St, 1–5 and 8–11 Green's Court including two famous specialist food shops, Lina's and Randall's, both long-established family businesses. The whole site is subject to compulsory purchase under a Westminster City Council slum clearance scheme, although Lina's and 22 Brewer St are 'added lands'; i.e. although in good condition they have been added to the scheme for more convenient redevelopment. Public enquiry 1972.

15 50–1 Berwick St, 195–7 Wardour St. **P.** Offices, shops, flats. **A.** Anthony Wylson, Munro and Waterston.
16 5, 6, 7 D'Arblay St. **P.** Offices, flats. **A.** H. Warren and Partners.
17 7 Poland St (listed). **P.** Offices, shops, flats. **A.** H. Warren and Partners.

18, Novello House

23, Kettner's

18 152–60 Wardour St (Pearson's Novello House of 1907 and factory behind but Novello House (listed) is to be retained). **P.** Office blocks, shops and flats. **A.** Sidney Kaye. **D.** Langholm Trust.
19. 83–5 Dean St, 1–8 St Anne's Court and 1b Richmond Buildings, owned by Westminster. **P.** 30,000 sq ft offices, shops, flats, car park. **A.** C. H. Elsom. **D.** Star (Great Britain).
20 9–12 St Anne's Court (continuous with above). **P.** Shops. **A.** B. Newton.
21 36–8 Dean St. **P.** Offices, restaurant, shops. **A.** Ronald Cox Associates. **D.** Stratton Estates.
22 47 Greek St. Formerly 'Boulangerie'. **P.** Offices, shops, flats. **A.** Covell Matthews and Partners.
23 13–17 Old Compton St, 40b Greek St and 26–32 Romilly St (Kettner's Restaurant and wine shop). **P.** 2 restaurants, 2 cinemas, flats. **A.** Richard Seifert. Gala Film Distributors have outline consent, but freeholders de Vere Hotels are reported to be acquiring property for a larger site.
24 Site bounded by Shaftesbury Avenue, Glasshouse St, Sherwood St and Denman St. The proposed redevelopment in fact extends up Great Windmill St to Ham Yard, with a realignment of Denman St to join Shaftesbury Avenue further north. This well-known site is part of the Piccadilly Circus scheme. Under the original application by Land Securities in

May 1972, planning permission was sought for a hotel, shops and flats on the site, part of which was still, at the end of 1972, owned by the GLC. Since the collapse of the scheme, it now seems likely that redevelopment will be mainly for offices, with shops and flats. **A.** Sir John Burnet Tait and Partners.
25 Site bounded by Piccadilly Circus, Lower Regent St, Jermyn St and Haymarket, including Criterion Theatre and Lillywhite's.

This site forms the southern part of the Piccadilly Circus scheme. Under the original application in May 1972, its owners Trust Houses Forte and architects Dennis Lennon and Partners hoped to redevelop the whole site for shops, restaurants and 214,000 sq ft offices. Controversy immediately centred on proposal to demolish the Criterion Theatre (1873, by Verity) and Westminster mounted pressure for the retention of both the Criterion and at least the facade of Lillywhite's. It is probable that these will be retained, and that the remainder of the site, bordering Coventry St, Haymarket, Jermyn St and Lower Regent St will be redeveloped.
26 Site bounded by Piccadilly Circus, Coventry St, Wardour St and Shaftesbury Avenue, including London Pavilion cinema (owned by GLC) the old Trocadero restaurant and the southern end of Rupert St.

Soho

26a, old Trocadero

26d, old Corner House

26b   26b, Monaco site; 26c, London Pavilion

26c

26e, Rupert St; 26f, Scott's Oyster Bar

26j, Chez Victor, Wardour St

26g, Gt Windmill St; 26h, Wardour St

26k, Garners, Wardour St

26i, Rupert Court

Forms by far the largest part of the Piccadilly scheme. Under the original application in May 1972, Stock Conversion and architects Fitzroy Robinson and Sidney Kaye sought permission for total redevelopment for 320,000 sq ft offices, plus shops and flats. Plans immediately aroused opposition, however, because of massive scale, and proposed destruction of a number of attractive, useful and interesting buildings — notably around Rupert Court, between Rupert St and Wardour St. A separate application had already been put in for the demolition of at least one listed building, the Garner's restaurant at 27 Wardour St. Under the various compromises put forward, it seems likely that some of the Stock Conversion site will be retained (including Rupert Court), although more of it will be redeveloped. Much of the area has for long been subject to 'developer's blight', involving for instance the closure of world-famous Scott's.

28a
28b

27a
27b

28a, Charing Cross Rd; 28b, Cambridge Circus

27a, Lisle St; 27b, Gerrard St

27 14–23 Lisle St, 36–43 Gerrard St (listed 18th-century buildings). Proposed extension to telephone exchange was turned down by Westminster in December 1972.

28 Site bounded by Shaftesbury Avenue, Newport Place, Newport Court and Charing Cross Rd (includes Sandringham flats West, a tenement block and music and book shops along Charing Cross Rd). Westminster is hoping to redevelop entire site up to Shaftesbury Avenue Fire Station, excluding Welsh Church, in conjunction with Trafalgar House. **P.** Offices, housing, shops and new fire station.

29 Site bounded by Shaftesbury Avenue, Wardour St, Gerrard St and Macclesfield St (part of 'Chinatown'). Most of block is being held by Stock Conversion for redevelopment.

30 Exeter Mansions. Owned by the GLC, who have warned tenants of eventual redevelopment, presumably on a site stretching back to Gerrard St.

31 North-east corner of Cambridge Circus (site bounded by Charing Cross Road, Phoenix St, St Giles's Passage and Shaftesbury Avenue also including western half of New Compton St and Stacey St). **P.** 16-storey block of offices (375,000 sq ft). **A.** Steane Shipman and Associates. **D.** Town and City.

31, Cambridge Circus

Soho

32

35
36

32 135–55 Charing Cross Rd (Edwardian offices and shops). **P.** 10-storey office block, shops, pedestrian arcades. **A.** Michael Lyell Associates. **D.** Amalgamated Investments.

33 Site bounded by Charing Cross Rd, Denmark St and St Giles's High St. Outline planning permission was granted in the early sixties to Sovneath Investments, a subsidiary of Harry Hyam's Oldham Estates, for a second phase of the Centre Point development. Although this is no longer active, there are signs of developer's blight in Denmark St and some proposal seems probable.

33, Corner of Charing Cross Rd and Denmark St

34 16–19 Soho Square, 9–15 Falconberg Mews. **P.** 24,700 sq ft offices, shops, 11,800 sq ft flats, industrial premises. **A.** Hanna and Mainwaring. **D.** Associated Suburban Properties.
35 127–31 Charing Cross Rd (Goslett's). Sterling Land seeking ODP for 40,000 sq ft offices.
36, 37 Discussions are going on between developers and Westminster about the future of two more sites on the north-east corner of Soho; the corner of Charing Cross Rd and Oxford St including Tottenham Court Rd underground station for a possible office tower block; and a site west along Oxford St. **D.** MEPC.

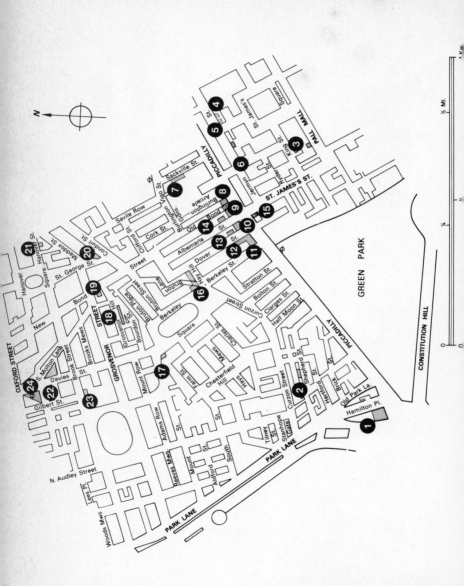

6. Mayfair

Hilton Hotel

The big changes in Mayfair took place between the wars, when the old town houses of the aristocracy down Park Lane and Piccadilly, and around Berkeley and Grosvenor Squares, were replaced by grandiose and featureless thirties piles. The main recent changes have been, firstly, the group of tourist hotels built at the southern end of Park Lane, led by the Hilton in 1962, and shortly to be joined by Stock Conversion's new hotel next to Apsley House; secondly, the new blocks along the south side of Oxford St, including two by Land Securities; and thirdly, the grim series of mainly government-occupied blocks around the top of Savile Row, including the aptly named Fortress House.

The centre of Mayfair, with its many remaining corners on a more intimate scale, is largely owned by the Grosvenor Estate, and is likely to remain comparatively unchanged. The two centres of new development are likely to be the north and the south. The Grosvenor Estate has come to an arrangement with Metropolitan Estates and Property Corporation (MEPC) for the redevelopment of almost all the older buildings remaining along the south side of Oxford St, west of Davies St. Westminster is favourable, and development is also likely on the Oxford St frontage, to the east, nearer Oxford Circus. There are several proposals for redevelopment in Bond St (the largest of them the Seifert-designed new block on the corner of Grafton St), and rumours of more in the offing. Hanover Square is now almost wholly dominated by comparatively recent developments, including Stock Conversion's Vogue House, and the new Capital and Counties block on the east side.

On the south there have been proposals for a continuous strip of modern development along the north side of Piccadilly from opposite the Ritz to the Burlington Arcade. Only Trafalgar House's replacement for the old Berkeley Hotel and the corner of Old Bond

Mayfair

St next to the Arcade have been agreed, and there are now pressures in Westminster Council to restrain such a complete transformation. A certain amount of redevelopment is taking place in Dover, Albemarle and Grafton Sts to the north. In St James's to the south, following such recent major schemes as the *Economist* building, Trafalgar House's Cleveland House headquarters in St James's Square, the neighbouring new Army and Navy Club, the new Cavendish Hotel and Seifert's Dunlop House in King St, proposed changes are comparatively small scale.

1 142–4 Piccadilly, 1–3 Hamilton Place. Demolished in 1972, after a public inquiry. Widely regarded as a test case, with bearing on the future possible redevelopment of St George's Hospital on the other side of Hyde Park Corner, since Apsley House is now rather absurdly isolated and the character of the area has finally been changed beyond recognition. **P.** Hotel. **A.** Frederick Gibberd and Partners. **D.** Stock Conversion.

2 22 Shepherd St (Carrington Dwellings). **P.** 10 storeys offices, flats. **A.** W. S. Hatchell.
3 55–8 Pall Mall, 2–5 Crown Passage (Edwardian offices). **P.** Shops, offices. **A.** Newman Levinson. Although this proposal has outline consent, Westminster is seeking to protect several other properties in the Pall Mall Conservation area, including 40–1, on which R. Seifert has an outstanding proposal for new offices.

4 and 5

7

7 29, 30, 30a Sackville St. Public inquiry was held at the end of 1972 over proposed demolition of these 18th-century listed buildings. **P.** Offices. **A.** Cubitt Nichols. **O.** Sutton Settled Estates.

4 105 Jermyn St (RSPCA). **P.** Shops, offices. **A.** T. P. Bennett and Son.
5 101–2 Jermyn St. **P.** Offices, flats. **A.** Chapman Taylor.

8

6. 91–2 Jermyn St (Turkish Baths). **P.** Conversion for offices, shops, sauna. **A.** R. Ward. **D.** Rochford Trust.

8 52–5 Piccadilly (next to Burlington Arcade). This and the next three sites are continuous down the north side of Piccadilly. **P.** Shops, offices, flats. **A.** R. Ward and Partners.

6

9, Piccadilly

12

12 38 Dover St. **P.** Offices, shops. **A.** Anthony Wylson and Munro Waterston.

9 56–62a Piccadilly, 45–50 Old Bond St and 1b and 2 Albermarle St (Triplex House and Qantas House). **P.** Offices and new Qantas Headquarters. **A.** Edward Stephan Associates. **D.** Qantas. Refused so far and subject to public inquiry. (See also 10.)

10 63–8 Piccadilly, 1 Dover St (National Westminster Bank and Calderhouse). **P.** Offices, shops, flats. **A.** Richard Seifert. Refused so far although compromise retaining bank facade is likely.

11 69–73 Piccadilly, 1–10 Dover Yard, 1–7 Berkeley St and 49 Dover St (old Berkeley Hotel site). **P.** Bristol Hotel, offices, shops. **A.** Chapman Taylor. **D.** Trafalgar House.

13

13 14 Dover St. **P.** Offices, flats. **A.** R. Ellis.

10a, Piccadilly; 10b, Dover St

10a

10b

Mayfair

14 9–10 Albermarle St. **P.** Offices, flats. **A.** Gollins, Melvin Ward.

15

15 50 St James's St (Devonshire Club). Planning permission for redevelopment was granted some years ago but has now expired. The club owners have put forward a new proposal for offices (architects, Mills Group Partnership) but it is unlikely that permission will be granted, unless the Club facade is to be retained.

16 1–4 Berkeley Square and 12 Hay Hill. Trafalgar House are hoping to develop this site for offices, but no formal application has yet been made.

16, Berkeley Square

17, Berkeley Square

17 34–5 Berkeley Square and 130 Mount St (listed). **P.** Offices. **A.** T. P. Bennett. Westminster was prepared to see these redeveloped, but owing to conservation pressure the Secretary of State for the Environment intervened to examine the proposal further.

18 Site bounded by Bourdon St, Grosvenor Hill and Broadbent St. Grosvenor Estate Strategy for Mayfair envisages redevelopment of this block (including tenement flats) for flats, offices and shops.

18, Grosvenor Hill

Mayfair

21 19–20 Hanover St. **P.** Offices, flats. **A.** Allerton, Rayner and Burroughs.

19

19 135–7 New Bond St (Aeolian Hall frontage). **P.** Offices, shops. **A.** Newman Levinson.
20 24–5 Conduit St, 36–7 George St. **P.** Offices, shops, **A.** Richard Seifert.

22

22 Site bounded by Davies St, South Molton Lane and Davies Mews (Boldings block). Leases on this site are being collected by Grosvenor Estate for redevelopment (presumably with MEPC — see 25 below).
23 73 Brook St. **P.** Offices.
24 Site bounded by Oxford St, Davies St, Weighhouse St and Gilbert St (formerly Grosvenor Palace Hotel and factory). Interior has already been gutted for new underground station for Fleet Line, and remainder will be redeveloped by MEPC when station reconstruction is complete.

continued on p. 80

24, Davies St

21

7. Victoria

Stag Place

This area ranges from the Cubitt and post-Cubitt squares and terraces of Belgravia and Pimlico in the north-west and south-west, through the glass and concrete towers of the New Victoria St, to the three huge slabs in Marsham St now the headquarters of the Department of the Environment. Much of the western half of the area was covered by the Grosvenor Estate's Strategy for Mayfair and Belgravia, prepared by architects Chapman Taylor in 1971.

Almost the whole of the central part of the Grosvenor Estate in Belgravia is not only a Conservation Area, but what the Estate calls a 'preservation area', meaning that in the foreseeable future almost no change will take place (the only exceptions being the current extension to the German Embassy in Chesham St, rebuilding in replica in Cliveden Place, and the important St George's Hospital site on the north-east corner).

In contrast, the main route from Buckingham Palace Rd, round the corner into Victoria St, and along to Parliament Square has already seen the beginning of one of the largest-scale redevelopments in London. The north side of Victoria St was subject to one of the major developments of the early sixties, extending from Buckingham Gate back through the Stag Brewery site to the new Gorringes store overlooking the gardens of Buckingham Palace. Now almost all the remaining parts of the original Victoria St are to follow suit, leaving the Albert Public house on the corner of Buckingham Gate and the block including the Victoria Palace theatre as the only older buildings in the street. One group which will particularly be missed is that around the south end of Buckingham Gate, including the grandly idiosyncratic Windsor House (to be replaced by a Seifert-designed tower block), and Windsor Street passage where small shops and restaurants are to be replaced by another tower block. Over 200 residents and shopkeepers were displaced at short notice by this development in the summer of 1972, with little hope of finding comparable premises in the area.

If some version of the huge scheme for Victoria Station comes to fruition, there will eventually be an almost continuous strip of post-1960 buildings all the way from Sloane Square to Westminster Abbey. Another area which will be transformed is the whole of the Vauxhall Bridge Rd, down to the huge Crown Estates scheme centred on Bassborough Gardens and surrounding streets.

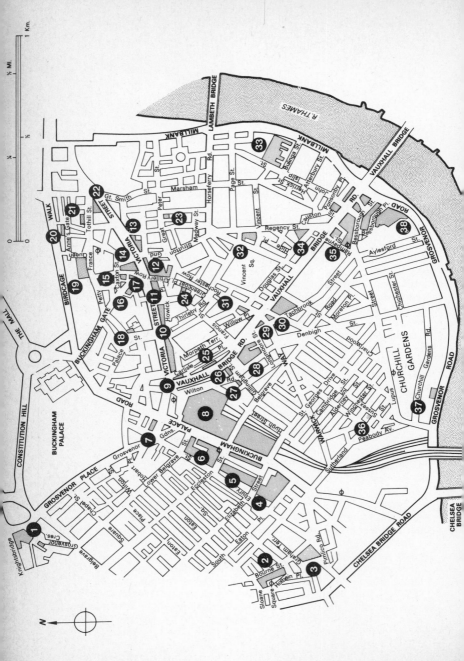

_a_
_b_   _1a, Grosvenor Crescent; 1b, Knightsbridge_

1   St George's Hospital, Hyde Park Corner. Described in the Grosvenor Estates' Strategy for Mayfair and Belgravia as 'one of the most important redevelopment opportunities in central London'. As long ago as 1943, the Abercrombie Plan spoke of the chance to redevelop the site with a building of 'national or international importance'.

The hospital building will be vacated by 1979. It was built in 1827 by Wilkins, architect of the National Gallery, University College and Grange Park, and is listed, although an alternative use may be hard to find. There will therefore be strong pressures both for and against demolition and considerable public controversy is likely.

A maximum area for redevelopment would also include 11–17 Knightsbridge and 11–15 Grosvenor Crescent.

1c, St George's Hospital

2a, Holbein Place

2   Sloane Square, east side. Bounded by Sloane Square, Holbein Place, Whittaker St, Bourne St and Cliveden Place. Grosvenor Estate envisage a two-phase development, beginning at southern end with redevelopment of Holbein Place, Whittaker St and Bourne St up to Skinner Mews, for shops and flats. Formal application Jan. 1973.

A longer-term phase two development, which would have to be in conjunction with the Cadogan Estates and other freeholders, would include the northern half of the block, through to Sloane Square (excluding Royal Court Theatre and new block over station).

2b, Bourne St; 2c, Sloane Sq

2b
2c

3a, Graham Terrace

4, Ebury St

3 Site bounded by Pimlico Rd, Passmore St, Bourne St and Graham Terrace. **P.** Flats, shops. **A.** Chapman Taylor. **D.** Grosvenor Estates.

4 Ebury St, south-east side. According to the Grosvenor Strategy, the houses and shops in the two blocks between Semley Place and Elizabeth St, and Eccleston St and Lower Belgrave St are in poor condition, and early redevelopment is being considered (see also 6).

5 Bounded by Buckingham Palace Rd, Ebury St, Eccleston St and Elizabeth St. An Office Development Permit has been granted for 200,000 sq ft offices to cover LEB substation in centre of this site. Porticoed Buckingham Palace Rd frontages (although listed) may be affected by road widening. Grosvenor Estate Strategy contemplates long-term redevelopment of Ebury St frontage.

3b-c, Bourne St

3b
3c

5, Buckingham Palace Rd

7

6a, St George's Baths

6 Bounded by Buckingham Palace Rd, Eccleston St, Ebury St and Lower Belgrave St (inc. St George's Baths and City Mission). **P.** £20 million scheme for 391,000 sq ft offices in 8-storey block, with 5-storey shops and flats on Ebury St. **D.** MEPC in conjunction with Grosvenor Estate.

7 Grosvenor Gardens (listed and in conservation area). Many buildings are being virtually rebuilt behind facades. Developers include Mackenzie Hill, Compass Securities and Chesterfield Properties. Architects include Chapman Taylor, and Gollins Melvin Ward. Possible redevelopment of block on south-east corner.

6b, Ebury St; 6c, City Mission 6b 8

8 Victoria Station. In 1968 the GLC promised a planning inquiry before any decision on the proposed rebuilding. Since then, nothing definite has been proposed.

6c

Victoria

12 Bounded by Victoria St, Artillery Place and Strutton Ground (including Artillery Mansions). Original proposal for 420,000 sq ft offices in exchange for agreement to build a hotel in Soho as part of the Piccadilly scheme, with T. P. Bennett and Sons as architects and Sir Basil Spence as consultant. For this Land Securities were going to buy the site for £4 million. Since original Piccadilly scheme was called in, the site will probably revert to Army and Navy (see above).

13

9-10, Victoria St

9 Corner of Victoria St, Vauxhall Bridge Rd, and Carlisle Place (National Westminster Bank site). **P.** New banking hall, 18,000 sq ft offices. **A.** C. H. Elsom Pack. **D.** National Westminster Bank.
10 Victoria St (south side) between Carlisle Place and Francis St. Three-acre site, a quarter of a mile long. **P.** £25 million scheme including 350,000 sq ft offices, 34 shops, flats, 155,000 sq ft car parking, banked on each side of piazza in front of Westminster Cathedral, and rising to towers 167 ft and 156 ft high. **A.** C. H. Elsom Pack. **D.** Chelwood Properties in conjunction with Church Commissioners.

13 Victoria St (south side) between Strutton Ground and Abbey Orchard. **P.** 200,000 sq ft offices. **A.** Trehearne and Norman Preston. **D.** Crown Commissioners and United Real Property.
14 Site between Victoria and Caxton Sts. Two of London's most individual Victorian blocks, Windsor Ho. (Pilkington 1881–3) and Iddesleigh Ho. (demolished Oct. 1972). **P.** Offices inc. 230-ft tower, shops, flats. **A.** Richard Seifert and Partners. **D.** Amalgamated Investments.

11

11 Army and Navy Stores, Victoria St. **P.** Department store with 10 floors offices above. **A.** C. H. Elsom Pack. **D.** Army and Navy Stores (14% owned by Amalgamated Investments who are bidding for control).

14a, Iddesleigh House

14b, Windsor House

16a

16b

15 Buckingham Gate (east side) behind Albert public house, through to Caxton St. Developers are retaining the Albert as a foil to their new block. **P.** 200-ft tower of office, flats. **A.** C. H. Elsom Pack. **D.** Amalgamated Securities.

15a, Buckingham Gate; 15b, Windsor Passage

16a-b, Hills Hygienic Bakery

16 60–1 Buckingham Gate (including Hills Hygienic Bakery by Verity 1887, in highly decorated pink terra cotta).
P. Offices, shops, flats. **A.** Chapman Taylor.
17 57 Buckingham Gate. **P.** Offices.
A. Howard Sant.
18 Palace St, Alexandra Buildings. Built in 1880s for Watney's employees, these model dwellings have been left stranded by redevelopment of Stag Brewery, and future seems highly uncertain.

15a

15b

18

19

25

19 Queen Anne's Mansions site, on corner of Queen Anne's Gate and Petty France. The *cause célèbre* of the summer of 1972. By the time drawings were published, planning permission had been granted, and despite national outcry the development has gone ahead. **P.** 250,000 sq ft offices (already pre-let to DOE) rising to 200-ft tower. **A.** Sir Basil Spence with Fitzroy Robinson and Partners. **D.** Land Securities.

20 Queen Anne's Gate (north-east side). 32,000 sq ft offices are being built behind facades and replicas by Amalgamated Investments.

21 Tothill Street, Caxton House. **P.** Offices, **D.** Commercial Union and British Land.

22 Corner of Victoria and Tothill St, Abbey). Built in 1860 as London's first 'luxury hotel', the Westminster Palace. Capital and Counties plan to redevelop with 150,000 sq ft offices in 1978.

23 69–71 Great Peter St. **P.** Shops, offices, flats. **A.** C. H. Elsom Pack.

24 22–4 Greencoat Place, **P.** Offices. **A.** Chapman Taylor. **D.** Greencoat Investments.

25 250–66 Vauxhall Bridge Road. **P.** Flats, offices, shops, pub. **A.** Michael R. Blampied and Partners. Scheme turned down on grounds of excessive office content.

26 8–14 Gillingham St. Various proposals for redevelopment, so far refused.

27 34–8 Gillingham St. **P.** Offices, shops, flats, warehouses.

28 Bounded by 211–33 Vauxhall Bridge Rd, Gillingham Row, Wilton Rd and Longmoore St. To be acquired by Westminster Council from Ministry of Defence as part of comprehensive redevelopment, for new swimming baths etc.

29 17–25 Tachbrook St and 183–91 Vauxhall Bridge Rd. **P.** Shops, offices, flats. **A.** Ronald Ward. Refused so far on grounds of excessive office content.

30a, Charlwood St; 30b, Tachbrook St

30 Bounded by Vauxhall Bridge Rd, Warwick Way, Tachbrook St and Charlwood St. Continuation of Council flats, northward from Lillington Garden Estate. Also scattered sites along other side of Vauxhall Bridge Rd, now derelict.

31 78–102 Rochester Row, 2 Willow Place. **P.** Shops, offices, flats. **A.** Chapman Taylor.

32 1–6 Fynes St, 3 Vincent Square, 56–74 Vincent St, 22–30 Regency St. **P.** Redevelopment for residential purposes.

Victoria

35b

35c

33 Queen Alexandra's Hospital, Millbank.
To be acquired in 1975 by Tate Gallery for
large extension.
34 102–10 Regency St, 26 Douglas St.
P. Warehousing, **A.** Leslie C. Norton.
D. Stock Conversion.
35 Bounded by Millbank, Grosvenor Rd,
Bessborough Place, Bessborough St,
Rampayne St, Vauxhall Bridge Rd,
Causton St and Ponsonby Place. On this
23-acre site the Crown Estates have a
conservation and redevelopment scheme
for 509 houses and flats, riverside walk
and 465,000 sq ft offices, including
Confederation of British Industry con-
ference centre. Streets to be wholly re-
developed include: Bessborough Gardens,
Bessborough Place, Bessborough St,
Dorset Place, Russell Place, north side of
John Islip St, west side of Ponsonby
Terrace and south side of Rampayne St.
Millbank Terrace may be retained.
A. Chapman Taylor. **D.** Crown Estates.

*35a, Bessborough Pl; 35b, John Islip St;
35c, Grosvenor Rd; 35d, Bessborough
Gdns; 35e, Bessborough St*

35a

35d

35e

36, Sutherland St

37

36   St Georges Estate, Pimlico. Since sale by Grosvenor Estate in 1952, this 42-acre early Victorian area has now been broken up. Only St George's Square, Warwick Square and Eccleston Square are protected by listing. Piecemeal redevelopment is beginning (e.g. Sutherland St and Sussex St) and considerably more seems likely. Developers include John Haskins and Co.

37   Grosvenor Rd, All Saints' Church (1871 by G. R. Cundy). Westminster may redevelop the site as an Old Peoples' Welfare Centre.
38   Grosvenor Rd, London Hydraulic Company Pumping Station (1875). The 1·35-acre site may be incorporated in Millbank Estate scheme (see 35).

Mayfair continued

Late entries (not on map)
25   MEPC in collaboration with Grosvenor Estate are to redevelop most of the remaining older buildings along the south side of Oxford St, between Davies St and Marble Arch.

25

26   32–3 St James's Place. **P.** Offices, flat. **A.** Douglas Feast.
27   41 St James's Place. Why have Westminster allowed scaffolding to remain on this listed building for 4 years? And why have they not used their powers to prevent its decay?
28   2–4 Waverton St (listed buildings). **P.** Houses. **Ap.** Debenham, Tewson and Chinnocks.

8. Whitehall to Temple

King's College, Strand

Although hardly a distinct 'area', this includes some of London's best-known riverside views along both banks of the Thames: from the Palace of Westminster, past Scotland Yard, Whitehall Court and County Hall, to the dignified classical facade of Somerset House. In the 1930s there were two notable developments on the north bank: the replacement of the old Cecil Hotel by Shell Mex House, and the demolition of Adelphi Terrace for the present Adelphi block. The Festival of Britain in 1951 initiated one of the most concentrated strips of post-War redevelopment in London along the south bank with clearance for the Festival site, and the Festival Hall. In the early sixties, on the site between Hungerford Bridge and County Hall, there arose the massive Shell Centre. In the mid-sixties, the old Shot Tower gave way to the Queen Elizabeth Hall and Purcell Room (opened 1967). In the late sixties, to the west, St Thomas's began its series of large new blocks across from the Houses of Parliament. To the east beyond Waterloo Bridge are the new headquarters of London Weekend Television, and the National Theatre by Denys Lasdun.

The most important likely changes in the next few years will be on the north bank. Firstly there will be the new parliament-extension building, next to Big Ben, and the breaking up of one of London's more attractive and useful jumbles of pubs, shops, houses and offices of many different designs and dates, to make way for other modern blocks. At the other end of Whitehall, another familiar London scene may be transformed by the two proposed new blocks on the south side of Trafalgar Square, while a question mark must hang over the rather shabby streets south of the Strand on each side of Charing Cross station.

At the other end of the Strand, almost any remaining older character is giving way before the combined onslaught of Kings College and the huge new Arundel Court development. Between them they will have carried off almost every vestige of one of London's most remarkable local architectural features — the late Victorian Gothic, and wide ornate porticos of John Dunn's hotels and offices on the Arundel Estate, north of Temple place. Kings College will also have demolished several handsome and curious buildings of the 17th, 18th and 19th centuries.

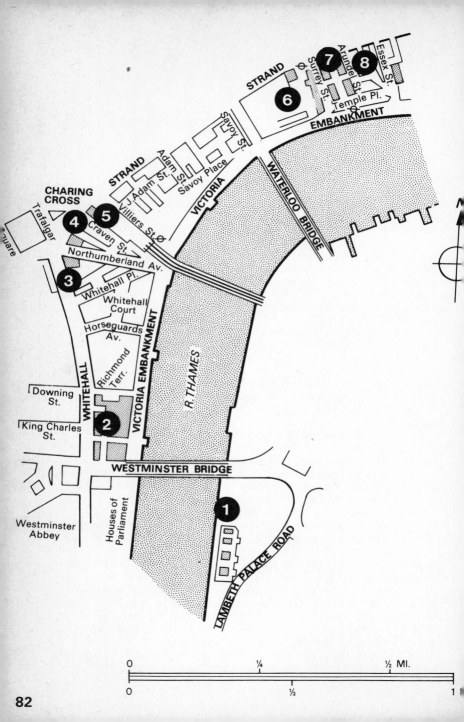

1 St Thomas's Hospital. The seven Italianate blocks by Currey (1868–71), with their campanile to the west, formed one of the best-known riverside views in London. Three blocks have already gone in St Thomas's present rebuilding pro-gramme, and the rest are to be covered in future phases.

2c, St Stephen's Tavern

2 Bounded by Whitehall, Richmond Terrace, Victoria Embankment and Bridge St. The future of the large group of build-ings at the south end of Whitehall, includ-ing the Georgian Richmond Terrace, the Whitehall Club and New Scotland Yard, was finally decided in November 1972 after years of discussion. The original proposal under the Martin-Buchanan plan of 1965 was for a complete redevelop-ment of the whole area. At a public inquiry in 1970, a powerful case was made for the retention of Richmond Terrace, the Whitehall Club and at least the north block of Norman Shaw's New Scotland Yard. Meanwhile plans went forward for the bronze-clad new Parlia-ment extension block on Bridge St, designed by Robin Webster and Robin Spence, which in itself will lie at the centre of one of the most photographed views in London, between Big Ben and Scotland Yard.

Following the Minister's decision of November 1972, the future of the area will be as follows: Richmond Terrace and

2a
2b

2a, Whitehall Club; 2b, Parliament St; 2d, Richmond Terrace

2d

83

Scotland Yard (north) are to be retained; the Home and Foreign Office blocks are to be rebuilt behind facades; and the remainder of the jumble of 18th- and 19th-century houses, pubs, offices and shops on the east side of Parliament St (Whitehall) will be replaced by a series of new government office blocks. Among the buildings to disappear will be the Italian pelazzo-style Whitehall Club (Parnell 1865); 43 and 44, built in 1753 (with fine interior features, including Chippendale staircase); St Stephen's Tavern; and the south block of New Scotland Yard (now thought to be also built to Shaw designs).

2, above, New Scotland Yard; below, Bridge St

3 and 4, Trafalgar Square

Whitehall to Temple

3 Trafalgar Square, corner of Whitehall and Northumberland Avenue (Trafalgar Buildings). **P.** 74,600 sq ft offices, 88-ft high. **A.** Richard Seifert. **D.** Amalgamated Investments for UK Provident Institution.

4 Trafalgar Square, corner of Northumberland Avenue, Strand and Northumberland St (Grand Buildings). This hive of one-room businesses with shopping arcade beneath was formerly the celebrated Grand Hotel (1878), the first in London at which it was respectable for married ladies to dine out. **P.** Offices rising to 140 ft. **A.** T. P. Bennett. **D.** Land Securities.

6b

5 Charing Cross Station forecourt. The £2 million scheme for reconstruction of Strand underground station (to be renamed Charing Cross) may involve the clearance of shops at the west end backing onto the Craven Hotel. Craven St: this decayed 18th-century street is partly listed. British Rail have no immediate plans for redevelopment.

6 Kings College, Strand. The College's extension programme has already involved the demolition in 1966 of the last two carved wooden-fronted 17th-century houses in the Strand, at 164–5. Its present redevelopment plans include: 152–8 the Strand; 21–35 Surrey St (including the Norfolk Hotel, and yellow-brick 18th-century houses at 33–4), the 17th-century Watch House over Strand Lane. **A.** Troupe and Steele. **D.** Kings College, London University.

6b, Strand Lane; 6c, Essex St

6c

6a, 152–8 Strand

7d

7a
7b

7c

7a-c, Demolished buildings on the Arundel estate; 7d, Strand

7 Bounded by Strand, Surrey St, Temple Place and Arundel St (including Norfolk St and Howard St). Until recently one of the more individual corners of late-Victorian London, with its streets of ornate red-brick hotels and offices by John Dunn on the Arundel Estate. These were demolished in 1970–2. **P.** Great Arundel Court, including 328,500 sq ft offices, 150 bedroom luxury hotel on Temple Place, in 5 blocks round a central open space. **A.** Frederick Gibberd and Partners. **D.** Capital and Counties, financed by Legal and General, and in association with Norfolk Family Estates.

8 32–4 Essex St (listed). 34 is 17th-century, 32 from mid-18th-century. A proposal by architects Powell and Moya for new offices, flats and barristers' chambers was turned down by Westminster in 1972.

9 36–9 Essex St and 2–3 Devereux Court. Richard Seifert had outline planning consent for offices, car park and flats, but the building was then 'spot-listed' and permission withdrawn in 1972. Under 'loophole' in planning legislation, no compensation could therefore be claimed (see under Suggestions).

9, Essex St

9. Covent Garden

New Winter Gardens

It has long been clear that the 100-odd acres of Covent Garden
face greater change than any other area in central London.

In 1968, following the decision to move the Market to Nine Elms,
the GLC published its Comprehensive Development Plan, a
pioneering attempt to co-ordinate the redevelopment of a whole area
of London by inviting private developers to work closely with the
GLC according to an overall plan (the GLC was even to buy 35 acres
by compulsory purchase in order to achieve this).

The Plan, with its open spaces, sunken roads, new housing and
office developments and a major new conference centre, involved
what the *Architectural Review* called 'a frightening amount of
destruction: certain destruction of buildings; probable destruction of
the social fabric'. More than 60% of the area was to be completely
rebuilt, including many historic buildings; 2000 people were to be
rehoused; several hundred small, often long-established businesses
probably dispersed.

When in January 1973 Geoffrey Rippon of the DOE approved
the Plan in principle, he did so with two major reservations. The first
was to knock out two of the particularly destructive new road
proposals, including the widening of Maiden Lane. The second was
to list an extra 250 buildings (originally 48 of the area's 82 listed
buildings were scheduled for demolition).

For all this, the question mark which still hangs over Covent
Garden is as large as ever. Encouraged by the GLC's comprehensive
approach, private developers have in recent years put forward many
schemes of their own (e.g. the 3-acre Odhams site on Long Acre).
Many of these will go through, although it is impossible to say at this
stage how far the GLC Plan will be amended in the next two years.

All the pictures on the following pages show buildings
threatened under the original plan, or by private proposals. Many
of them have since been listed, but this will not automatically mean a
permanent reprieve.

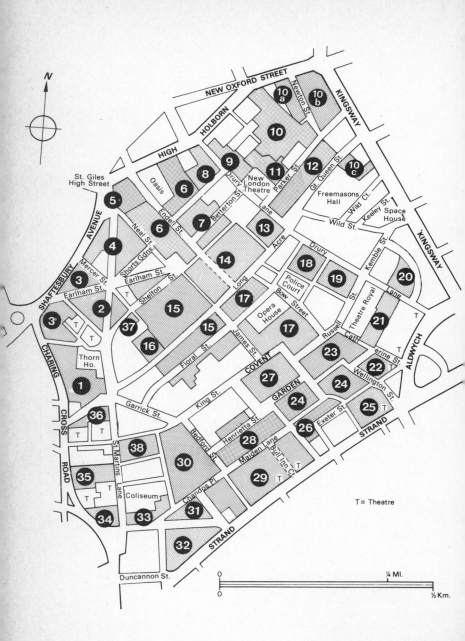

1a-b, Charing Cross Rd

1c

1 Bounded by Charing Cross Rd, Litchfield St, St Martin's Lane, Cranbourne St (including the whole of Gt Newport St, but excluding Cranbourne Chambers). The main part of the area is Sandringham Flats East on the Charing Cross Rd. Owners GLC plan to rehabilitate the flats for another ten years use. Town and City who own frontages on Gt Newport St, including Arts Theatre Club, have said that they plan office and shop development for the whole site, although this is somewhat embarassing to the GLC who must regard such proposals as premature.

1c, Gt Newport St; 1d, the Cranbourne pub; 1e, Smith's shop in Charing Cross Rd

1d

1e

Covent Garden

2a   2b

2a, Tower Court; 2b, Monmouth St

2 Area between Earlham St, Tower St, Shelton St and Mercer St (including Georgian shops in Tower Court and many long-established businesses). Major owners: Stock Conversion, Comyn Ching. Zoned under Plan for Sports and Recreation.

3 Frontage to Charing Cross Rd and Shaftesbury Avenue between Litchfield St and Mercer St. Cambridge Circus corner including Marquis of Granby pub. The whole area is zoned for private housing, shops and offices. Richard Seifert applied on behalf of Amalg. Investments for offices and luxury flats on site bounded by 15–27 Earlham St, 164 Shaftesbury Avenue and 33–43 Mercer St, but withdrew pending DOE decision.

4 Site bounded by Shaftesbury Avenue, Neal St, the west half of Shorts Gardens and Mercer St (including Upper Monmouth St). GLC own freeholds on Shaftesbury Avenue corner of Monmouth St and propose to buy French Hospital (Verity, 1899). Gower St Memorial Chapel on corner of Shaftesbury Avenue and Mercer St is owned by Stock Conversion. Zoned for offices, housing.

5 76–82 Neal St, 190–204 Shaftesbury Av. 73–81 Endell St (including Swiss Church and school). Amalgamated Investments hope to redevelop whole block, although Swiss Church recently listed.

6 Bounded by Neal St, Shelton St, parts of Endell St and through to High Holborn (including Cross Keys Public House and Latchford's Timber Yard). Zoned for council housing, shops, health centre, hotel and offices. Several recent listings including Dudley House, Shorts Gardens.

3, Charing Cross Rd

6a-b, Endell St

6a

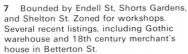

7a, Endell St; 7b, Betterton St

7 Bounded by Endell St, Shorts Gardens, and Shelton St. Zoned for workshops. Several recent listings, including Gothic warehouse and 18th century merchant's house in Betterton St.

8 Bounded by High Holborn, Drury Lane and Shorts Gardens. Being redeveloped by Haslemere Estates (architect Geoffrey Spire) for offices, hotel and hostel.

9 Frontages on Drury Lane and Macklin St (including White Hart public house). Zoned for council housing and shops. Recent listings including 17th century panelled interior at 187 Drury Lane.

10 and **11** Irregular site with frontages on Drury Lane, Gt Queen St, Parker St, Macklin St, Newton St, and through to Holborn Town Hall on High Holborn. Zoned for Camden housing, primary school. Recent listings include Town Hall.

10a 199–206 High Holborn, 2–8 Newton St. **P.** Offices, flats (replacing shops on High Holborn). **A.** Richard Seifert. **D.** MEPC.

10b 207–19 High Holborn, 1–29 Newton St, 45–51 Parker St, and Kingsway frontages. Plans for major developments by Newton St Investments (50% owned by MEPC) upset by recent listing of Princess Louise pub. New proposals expected.

10c Kingsway Hall (finest recording studio in London). Recently sold by Methodists and future uncertain.

10a, Holborn Town Hall

10b, Newton St

14, Odhams site

12, Gt Queen St

trump card has been outline planning permission for 12-storey block on west half of the site. Unless his new proposals are accepted he has threatened to implement his old permission by building large tower block.

15   Victorian warehouses, offices, pubs, and shops largely connected with the market, stretching from Earlham St, through to Floral St. Zoned for council housing, shops, workshops, play areas, offices and open space.

15a, Long Acre; 15b, Shelton St; 15c, Langley St

12   Bounded by Parker St, Newton St, and Gt Queen St. **P.** Offices and flats. Possible redevelopment by MEPC for Freemasons.

13   Bounded by Drury Lane and Long Acre. To be redeveloped on behalf of freeholders, Mercers' Company.

14   Bounded by Long Acre, Arne St, Shelton St and Neal St (including southern end of Endell St and Dryden St). This 3·2 acre site is the largest in Covent Garden. The Odham's building on the corner of Endell St was demolished in July 1972. **P.** 200,000 sq ft offices, 30 luxury flats, 30 'low income' flats. **A.** Richard Seifert. **D.** MEPC in association with IPC. This huge £20 million scheme has been the subject of argument between the GLC and Seifert, whose

15a

15b

17a

17a, Nag's Head; 17b, Floral Hall

16 Site bounded by Long Acre, Slingsby Place and Mercer St. Zoned for housing and studios (to be compulsorily purchased by GLC).

17 Large irregular site to north-west and south of Royal Opera House. Includes Nag's Head public house and Floral Hall (1859) by E. M. Barry, both recently listed. Various extensions to the Opera House still not settled (architects Gollins, Melvin Ward), but whole area has been zoned for this.

18 and **19** Victorian tenement blocks on Drury Lane. Zoned for council housing and telephone exchange.

20 Tenement blocks on Kean St and Drury Lane, owned by Westminster, to be demolished for road widening.

21 Site to south of Theatre Royal between Drury Lane and Catherine St. GLC council flats, vacated 1972. **P.** Waldorf Hotel extension. **D.** Trust Houses Forte.

22 Bounded by Tavistock St, Catherine St, Exeter St and Wellington St (including Duchess Theatre). Zoned for road widening, restaurant and new theatre (by private developer after acquisition by the GLC).

15c

17b

23a

23b

25a

25b

23a, Wellington St; 23b, Tavistock St

25a-b, Strand; 25c, Lyceum Theatre

23 Bounded by Russell St, Catherine St, Tavistock St and Covent Garden Market (including part of Bow St). Zoned for International Conference Centre, shops and pub, by a private developer in association with GLC. Includes 18th-century houses where Johnson met Boswell and de Quincey wrote the *Opium Eater*.

24 Bounded by Tavistock St, Exeter St and Wellington St (including market building and part of present flower market). Zoned for shops and hotel by private developer in association with GLC.

25 Bounded by the Strand, Burleigh St, Exeter St and Wellington St (including Lyceum Theatre, portico 1831 by Samuel Beazley and 356—9 Strand, by Nash). Zoned for offices, hotel and entertainment facilities by private developer in association with GLC.

25c

24, Wellington St

26, Flower Market

27b

27a-b, Fowler's Market buildings

26 Site bounded by Southampton St, Tavistock St and Covent Garden Market (including western half of Flower Market). Zoned for offices, flats, shops by a private developer in association with the GLC.

27 Covent Garden Piazza, including central Market buildings by Fowler (1828–31). Private developers, including Haslemere Estates, have been interested. It seems likely that most of the structure, which is listed, will be retained, possibly for cafes, boutiques etc., although the cast-iron and glass roof will probably disappear. Originally the piazza (by Inigo Jones) was an arcaded open space fronting the false porch of St Paul's church. The Duke of Bedford placed the market buildings in the centre of London's first and once most fashionable residential square in 1828, and it has been suggested that Jones's original arcade might be reconstructed.

28 Henrietta St and Maiden Lane. Both streets would have been largely demolished to make way for 'southern spine road' (now dropped). Their future therefore remains uncertain.

28, below, Henrietta St; overleaf, a, Chandos Pl; b, Garrick's house (saved?)

27a

Covent Garden

29a, Strand; 29c, Strand

28a
28b

29   Bounded by Maiden Lane, Agar St, the Strand and Southampton St (including Bedford St, Exchange Court and Bull Inn Court). The longest stretch of the Strand untouched by recent development including the Vaudeville Theatre, recently listed. Buildings from the last three centuries and old alley ways off the Strand. Parts of the site including Adelphi Theatre and Civil Service Stores are owned by Country and New Towns who hope for comprehensive redevelopment with offices and shops, possibly in conjunction with another developer.

29b, Exchange Court

29c

30c

30 Bounded by Bedford St, New Row, Bedfordbury and Chandos Place (including Moss Bros., Dents the publishers and Peabody Estate tenements. Zoned for offices, small shops and flats by a private developer in association with GLC.

30a-b, Bedford St; 30c, New Row; 30d, Bedford Court

30a
30b

30d

Covent Garden

31

33, King William IV St

33 Bounded by St Martins Lane (south of Coliseum), King William IV St, Chandos Place and Bedfordbury. Zoned for offices by a private developer in association with the GLC.
34 Old Westminster City Hall and National Westminster site facing Edith Cavell's statue. To be redeveloped by GLC as new municipal library.

31 Charing Cross Hospital, Agar St. To be redeveloped for hotel and entertainment facilities by a private developer in association with GLC, retaining porticoed facade on Agar St (by Decimus Burton 1831–54).
32 Triangular site bounded by the Strand, Adelaide St and King William IV St. Part of Nash's West Strand Improvement scheme executed by Robert Smirke. After controversy in late 1960s Nash's 'Pepperpots' and stuccoed facades on corners are to be retained but whole interior is to be re-built with modern frontages in the centre of each side.
P. Offices, shops, new bank. **A.** Frederick Gibberd and Partners. **D.** Coutts.

34, above and below, Charing Cross Rd

32, Coutts Bank

35, Mansion blocks, St Martin's Lane

38, New Row

35   Between Charing Cross Rd, north of Garrick Theatre and St Martin's Lane. To be redeveloped on behalf of GLC and Gascoyne-Cecil Estates.

36   Between Charing Cross Rd and St Martins Lane fronting Cranbourne St. Zoned for office and shop redevelopment by a private developer in association with the GLC.

37   On corner of Shelton St and Mercer St including Mercer's Arms public house. Owners, David Lewis Group, evacuated tenants from these properties in 1972, despite protests, although future of the site had not yet been agreed with GLC.

38   Site bounded by St Martins Lane, New Row, Bedfordbury and Hop Garden Row. Although zoned for retention a certain amount of piecemeal development seems possible.

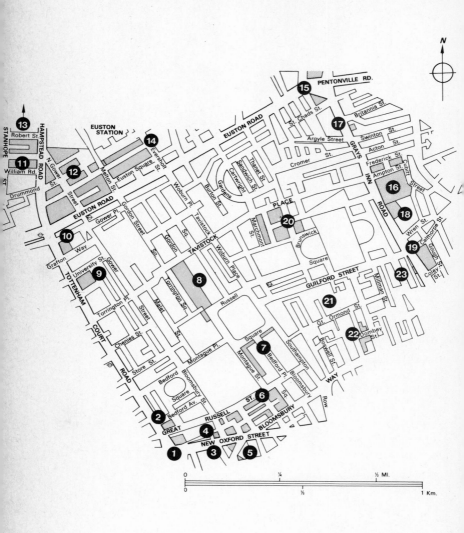

University College Theatre

10. Bloomsbury and Camden

The heart of the area is 18th and early 19th-century Bloomsbury
bounded by Tottenham Court Rd, Euston Rd, Grays Inn Rd and
High Holborn. At the north-west corner, towering over Euston Rd
and Hampstead Rd, stands the largest of all speculative developments
in the post-war London, Joe Levy's Euston Centre. Other notable
recent developments further along the Euston Rd are the Hearts of
Oak gold-tinted-glass tower; Camden's cultural centre; and the new
Euston station. To the east, in Grays Inn Rd, stands Lord Thomson's
copper palace (1963); to the south, the already shabby, discoloured
blocks of the late fifties (by Seifert) bridging Proctor St, while in
Bloomsbury itself are London University's various modernistic
intrusions into the Georgian squares and terraces; the glass ziggurat
off Brunswick Square; and the large concrete box which has replaced
the riotous Edwardian extravaganza of the old Imperial Hotel in
Russell Square (demolished 1966).

  The most notable development in central Bloomsbury is the
continuing demolition of Woburn Square (two groups of the elegant
late-Georgian houses and Vulliamy's Christ Church were still standing
at the end of 1972).

  On the edge of the area are four or five developments on a much
vaster scale. With his holdings in the Tolmers Square area, and to
the east of Kings Cross station, Joe Levy is hoping for two big new
office developments and the Kings Cross area is likely to see great
change. Grays Inn Rd will be transformed by the new Lyon and
Seifert/*Times* development on the east side, while the proposed
razing of streets south of the British Museum for the monolithic
National Library remains deservedly one of the most controversial
schemes mooted since the War.

Bloomsbury and Camden

1 Dominion Cinema, Tottenham Court Rd. The Rank Organisation hopes to redevelop for offices.
2 Bounded by Tottenham Court Rd, Great Russell St, Adeline Place and Bedford Avenue. New YMCA building.
3 Bounded by New Oxford St, Bloomsbury St, Streatham St and Dyott St. (including Giddon's 18th-century warehouse and Adam room). **P.** Offices, shops, flats. **D.** Town and City. Refused in 1972, although new proposals likely.

1

4, Bloomsbury St

4 65 New Oxford St (Albion House block). **P.** 50,000 sq ft offices.
5 Shaftesbury Theatre, Princes Circus. Peureula Investments paid £1.16 million for site in 1972. Redevelopment likely.
6 Bounded by Bloomsbury St, New Oxford St, Great Russell St through to Bloomsbury Square, including Museum St, Coptic St, Little Russell St and Bury St, excluding listed buildings. This 7½-acre jumble of streets includes pubs such as the Museum Tavern, many small shops, including bookshops, Craddock and Barnard's gallery and Cameo Corner; restaurants, publishers' offices, and flats at reasonable rental for 600 people. For years the area has provided a centre for visitors to the British Museum from all over the world. **P.** The massive £36 million National Library

5

6a
6b

102

6c 6d

6a, New Oxford St; 6b, Gt Russell St;
6c, Museum St; 6d, Coptic St

scheme to include the British Museum
and other national libraries. The scheme
is the responsibility of the Department of
Education and Science. Work is scheduled
in two phases, starting in late 1973,
although in 1972 Camden were still
objecting to the scheme on the grounds
that it will displace 600 people.

7 Russell Square (south side). In 1972
Bedford Estates appealed to the Minister
over refusal to allow redevelopment.

8 Woburn Square and Russell Square
(north west). London University's expansion into Bloomsbury continues. In 1959
Sir Leslie Martin published his plan for the
next phase of rebuilding in the 18th- and
early 19th-c. terraces and squares which
made up one of the finest town-planning
compositions in the world. Although this
caused comparatively little stir at the
time, when the plans for the demolition of
Woburn Place emerged again in 1968–9

7

8a, Russell Square; 8b, Christ Church,
Woburn Square

8a 8b

103

8c, Woburn Square

10

11, Hampstead Rd

12a

there was a major public outcry. London University were able to produce outline planning permission granted years before, however, and the destruction is going ahead. Demolition of Woburn Square has already begun, but the time and full extent of the destruction is not yet known. The future of Christ Church, Woburn Square (Lewis Vulliamy 1831) remains uncertain.

9 Bounded by Tottenham Court Rd, University St and Capper St. Appeal outstanding on Sir Max Rayne's proposal for 40,000 sq ft offices, workshops, flats and hospital accommodation.

10 Maples department store. Demolished at end of 1972. **P**. 60,000 sq ft offices, flats, laboratory space for UCH. **A**. R. Seifert **O**. Maples-Macowards.

12b

Bloomsbury and Camden

12c

12d
12e

11   Bounded by Hampstead Rd, Robert
St and Drummond St. **P.** Housing, school
(Tolmers Square Phase I). **D.** Camden
Council.
12   Bounded by Hampstead Rd, Euston
Rd and Melton St, including Tolmers
Square, North Gower St, Euston St,
Drummond St, Stephenson Way, Starcross
St and Cobourg St. 15-acre area, including Georgian terraces, restaurants, shops,
offices. Stock Conversion have recently
concluded a highly advantageous deal
with Camden, to provide housing at back
of site, in return for Euston Centre-type
office development on Euston Rd.

12f

*12a-b, North Gower St; 12c, Drummond
St; 12d, Tolmer Cinema; 12e, Tolmers
Square; 12f, Hampstead Rd*

13   Camden High St, including Camden Theatre. Camden are engaged in a study of entire area, with view to eventual large-scale redevelopment. Stock Conversion own the Camden Theatre.

14   Euston Station, forecourt. Plans for 405,000 sq ft offices designed by Richard Seifert still under discussion with GLC and Camden Council. If the offices (equivalent to two Centre Points) are built in tower-block form they will only occupy the immediate forecourt. If, as Camden prefers, they are built in lower profile, they will cover the existing gardens on Euston Square. **D.** British Rail.

13

15   Kings Cross station and surrounding area. Massive redevelopment in the near future is likely. 1. Kings Cross station (by L. Cubitt 1851) is likely to be terminal for the new third London airport, probably involving major rebuilding, to include large office content. Station is listed but may be treated as expendable, in exchange for retention of the more impressive St Pancras next door, which Camden want for a leisure-centre. 2. The decayed groups of mid-Victorian buildings around the Kings Cross cinema will be demolished as part of the GLC's big new road-widening and roundabout scheme at the top of Grays Inn Rd. 3. Joe Levy's Stock Conversion has acquired sites between Pentonville and Wharfedale Rd, for major office development. 4. British Rail is hoping to sell off or redevelop some of the large area of land north of the two stations, in Somers Town and goods yards. 5. 188–208 Pentonville Rd. **P** 159,000 sq ft offices in 2 towers. **A.** Chapman Taylor **D.** Sterling Land.

15

15

16, Ampton St

Bloomsbury and Camden

19　Bounded by Grays Inn Rd, Gough St, Calthorpe St and Coley St. **P.** 490,000 sq ft offices and works. **A.** Richard Seifert. **D.** Thomson Newspapers (for *The Times*, when it moves from Printing House Square). Demolition of listed Georgian terrace 6–24 Calthorpe St so far refused.

20　Bounded by Brunswick Square, Tavistock Place, Marchmont St, and Bernard St. Marchmont Properties 'banked greenhouse' development, including offices, hotel 40,000 sq ft shopping and 558 homes for Camden Council (original plan by Sir Leslie Martin). The southern half is built. Completion up to Tavistock Place prevented because terms for surrender of drill hall in Handel St unacceptable to Territorial Army.

16　Bounded by Frederick St, Cubitt St, Ampton St and Grays Inn Rd, and open space south of Ampton St, including terraces in Frederick St, Cubbitt St and Ampton St by Thomas Cubitt. (Calthorpe Estate). **P.** 70,000 sq ft offices, warehousing, showrooms, housing. **D.** Ronald Lyon. Some of the few remaining Cubitt facades are to be preserved.

17　300–6 Grays Inn Rd. **P.** Offices, shops. **A.** Sidney Kaye. **D.** Stock Conversion.

18　Royal Free Hospital and Dental Hospital, Grays Inn Rd. When Royal Free moves up to Hampstead, and Dental Hospital to Paddington, this site will be freed for redevelopment, although no plans published as yet (possibly to be included in Lyon scheme, see 16 above).

21, Lansdowne Terrace

21　Area north of High Holborn, including Great Ormond St, Millman St, Lansdowne Terrace, Guilford St (19th-century terraces built on marshes of Fleet). Recently, the various owners, including Derby and Rugby Estates, have had considerable problems with collapse through subsidence. Many houses already demolished, including east side of Millman St, to be used for council housing. Many are listed, or have preservation orders, which has involved owners in disproportionately costly preservation schemes. The long-term future of the area must remain highly uncertain.

18

22   Dombey St, Harpur St, Ordehall St.
Boarded-up for several years but there are
said to be plans for rehabilitation by the
Harpur Trust.
23   131 Grays Inn Rd (Blue Lion pub)
P. Flats and new pub. **A.** Sir John
Burnet Tait and Partners. **D.** Truman's. On
appeal to D.O.E.

22, Dombey St

Press Centre,
Shoe Lane (Seifert)

11. Kingsway to Ludgate Hill

From Lincoln's Inn in the north-west, this district stretches down its
two main thorough-fares, Holborn and Fleet St to gloomy, narrow
corridors of 19th- and 20th-century offices in the east, interspread
with islands of character. The most obvious recent redevelopments
have been along Holborn: State House (by Trehearne and Norman
Preston, 1959), National Westminster House, the _Daily Mirror_
building on New Fetter Lane (1963); with, tucked away between
Carey St and Portugal St, Seifert's Inland Revenue block for Harry
Hyams. The demolition of the Georgian terraces at the south-west
corner of Lincoln's Inn Fields was one of the conservationist _causes
célèbres_ of the late fifties.

The area between Holborn and Fleet St is presently being
subjected to a blitz of redevelopment, led by Seifert's Press Centre
on the east, which in turn will be dwarfed by Capital and Counties
vast proposed block on Wine Office Court, dominating the whole
Fleet St area. W. H. Smith's new 12-storey headquarters at the
north end of Fetter Lane can but improve what is already almost the
most dreary spot in London, but the three new developments at the
south end will transform a familiar view, looking up from Fleet St
past the corner where a Peele's Hotel has stood since 1518. On
Holborn itself the main proposal is the huge new Seifert scheme on
the Gamages site, including the demolition of half Hatton Garden,
while further proposals are in the air for some of the remaining older
buildings on the south side of Holborn.

Some of the alleys off Fleet St itself are undergoing considerable
change, notably the disappearance of Racquet Court and 'Poppins'
pub, demolished in 1972; Crane and Wine Office Courts; the Feathers
pub, demolished in 1971 (although none likely to cause so much
stir as the threat to Fleet St's best known drinking haunt, El Vino's).
Several of the larger and more interesting 19th-century buildings in
the south-east, by the Embankment, are likely to disappear (notably
the bizarre City of London Boys School, and possibly the handsome
Bridewell Hospital facade).

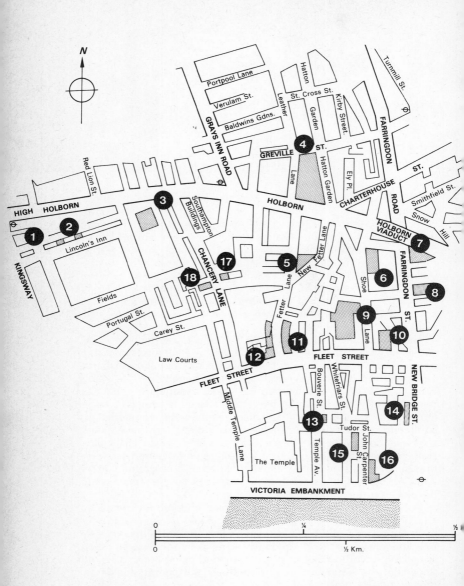

N

Portpool Lane
Verulam St.
Baldwins Gdns.
GRAYS INN ROAD
Leather
Hatton
St. Cross St.
Garden
Kirby Street.
Turnmill St.
FARRINGDON
GREVILLE
St.
4
Hatton Garden
Lane
Ely Pl.
CHARTERHOUSE
ROAD
St.
HOLBORN
Smithfield St.
Snow
Hill
Red Lion St.
3
Southampton
Buildings
HOLBORN
VIADUCT
HIGH   HOLBORN
2
7
1
Lincoln's Inn
CHANCERY   LANE
17
5
New Fetter Lane
6
FARRINGDON
KINGSWAY
18
Fetter Lane
8
Shoe
Lane
9
Fields
Portugal St.
Carey St.
11
10
Law Courts
12
FLEET   STREET
ST.
FLEET   STREET
Bouverie St.
Whitefriars St.
NEW
BRIDGE
ST.
Middle Temple Lane
13
14
Tudor St.
John Carpenter
St.
The Temple
Temple Av.
15
16

VICTORIA   EMBANKMENT

0   ¼   ½
0   ½ Km.

110

Kingsway to Ludgate Hill

1 **1** 3–4 Lincoln's Inn Fields. **P.** Offices. **D.** Compass Securities.

2 10–11 Lincoln's Inn Fields. **P.** Offices. **A.** Brian Westwood. **D.** Equity and Law. The above two prestige office developments will be the first two modern intrusions into the Georgian terrace on the north side of Lincoln's Inn Fields, although in each case the buildings they replace were Victorian.

3 North Lawn, Lincoln's Inn. Trustees awaiting decision from the Minister over proposal for 73,000 sq ft offices on the edge of this lawn.

4 Bounded by Holborn, Leather Lane, Greville St and Hatton Garden (including Gamages). **P.** 320,000 sq ft offices, shops, new department store, housing, piazza, workrooms for diamond trade. **A.** Richard Seifert. **D.** Sterling Guarantee and Town City.

Controversy has centred on the displacement of a large part of Hatton Garden jewellery trade, and offer of new premises at considerably inflated rents.

5 Site bordering Fetter Lane, New Fetter Lane and Plough Place. **P.** 12 storey headquarters for W. H. Smith and Son. **A.** Casson, Conder and Partners.

2

4a-b, Hatton Garden; 4c, Gamages

4a   *4b*

4c

6   Shoe Lane. Oldbourne Hall and
Evening Standard building, shortly to be
vacated when new premises next to
Daily Express are complete.   **P.** Offices.
A. Dennis Lennon and Partners.
D. Beaverbrook Properties.
7   14–23 Holborn Viaduct and 37–40
Farringdon St. Holborn Viaduct was
constructed in 1863–9 to the design of
Horace Jones. Two of its four Italianate
structures remain, containing broad
stairways to the viaduct, but both are
now threatened.   **P.** 110,000 sq ft
offices rising to 9 storeys over Viaduct
and 12 over Farringdon St.   **A.** T. P.
Bennett and Sons.   **D.** Holborn Viaduct
Land Co. (subsidiary of Central and
District Properties).

6

7

8, Farringdon St

8   22–5 Farringdon St and 1–2 Bear
Alley (Fleetway House).   **P.** Offices, car
parking.   **D.** Amalgamated Investments.
A more satisfactory site would include the
two buildings to the north of Fleetway
House, and these may be included in the
eventual development.
8a   88 Farringdon St.   **P.** Offices.
D. Amalgamated Investments.
9   Bounded by Wine Office Court, Shoe
Lane and Little New St.   **P.** 20 storey
block offices, with pub on Shoe Lane,
totalling 280,000 sq ft (twice bulk of
nearby Press Centre).   **A.** Ronald Fielding
Partnership.   **D.** Capital and Counties.
10   Bounded by Fleet St and Poppins
Court, including Racquet Court (18th-
century houses and Red Lion pub – 'the
Poppins'). The Red Lion was demolished
October 1972.   **P.** Extension of *Daily
Express* building, to accommodate
Evening Standard.   **A.** Ellis Clarke and
Gallannaugh.   **D.** Beaverbrook Properties.

10, Poppins Court

11 Corner of Fleet St and Fetter Lane (east). A large site backing on to Crane Court, extending up Fetter Lane to Fleur-de-Lis Court, and including old Peele's Hotel, is being assembled here by Consolidated Securities for office redevelopment. **A.** Julian Keyes Partnership.

12 Corner of Fleet St and Fetter Lane (west) up to Hen and Chickens Court. Future of these properties uncertain, although Compass Securities involved.

12a Fetter Lane. St Dunstan's House. To be redeveloped for DOE.

13 Tudor St, Feathers public house (demolished 1972). **P.** Offices. **A.** Royce Topping Hurley and Stewart. **D.** Associated Newspapers.

12, Fleet St

11a, Fleet St/Fetter Lane; 11b, Peele's Hotel

14 13–18 New Bridge St, 2–4 Tudor St, 9–12 Bridewell Place (including Court Room of Bridewell Royal Hospital, 1802–5). **P.** Offices. **A.** Richard Seifert. **D.** Governors of Bridewell Hospital. Outline permission for redevelopment was granted some years ago. Hospital since listed. Permission to demolish was refused. Richard Seifert's appeal still with Minister (although detailed drawings have been submitted).

14, Bridewell Hospital

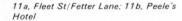

11a
11b

15

16

17

15 John Carpenter St, Guildhall School of Music (Horace Jones, 1885–7), and City of London Girls School, Carmelite St. These are moving to Barbican, and sites will be redeveloped on behalf of City of London Corporation for offices and car parking.

16 City of London Boys School, Victoria Embankment (1881–2). The school is to be moved a few hundred yards to the east, next to the Mermaid Theatre, and the site redeveloped on behalf of the City of Corporation for offices and car parking.

Late Entries (not on map)
17 22 Chancery Lane. To be re-developed by estate agents Weatherall Green for their own use.
18 78–89 Chancery Lane, 8–14 Bishops Ct., 1–17 and 2–12 Chichester Rents (inc. listed bldgs.) **P.** Offices, shops, flats **A.** Trehearne Norman Preston. **D.** Stock Conversion.
19 39–43 Fleet St (inc. El Vino's wine bar). **P.** 60,000 sq ft offices, flats. **A.** Devereux and Ptnrs. **D.** MEPC (in conjunction with Hoare's Bank, Norwich Union and El Vino).

12. The City

Barbican

Apart from Covent Garden, the City faces more intensive change than any other area of London. During the War more than a third of 'the square mile' was razed by bombs, particularly the north west and around St Paul's. During the sixties, it was these areas which saw most of the large-scale redevelopment, notably the St Paul's Precinct by William Holford (1964) and the five 18 storey curtain-wall towers along Route II (London Wall), comprising the first phase of the Barbican scheme. By the late sixties, the trouble-plagued second phase of the Barbican scheme was under way to the north, with its towers of flats and new Arts Centre.

More recently the focus of redevelopment has changed to the south and east. Here the way was led by Seifert's 28-storey National Provincial tower in Drapers Gardens (1967) and the rebuilding of the domed Victorian Stock Exchange with its 321-ft tower. The City Corporation's elaborate plan for a 'city of the future' includes a complex of elevated walkways. The pace of redevelopment is now such that within twenty years only little, carefully protected pockets of older buildings are likely to remain.

By the end of 1972, much of the City along the Thames had been demolished for the new southern through-route along the lines of Upper and Lower Thames St (which will eventually stretch from Blackfriars to Billingsgate Market). Further north, one of the few remaining predominantly Victorian thoroughfares, Eastcheap, faces large-scale redevelopment. Another huge building site was opening up in 1972 along almost the whole western side of Bishopsgate, which will be dominated by two huge new Seifert towers. To the north again, the Victorian stations of Broad St and Liverpool St are likely to follow Blackfriars and Cannon St (another probable Seifert scheme), while a large area in the north-east was at the end of 1972 still subject to 'study' by the City planners, in

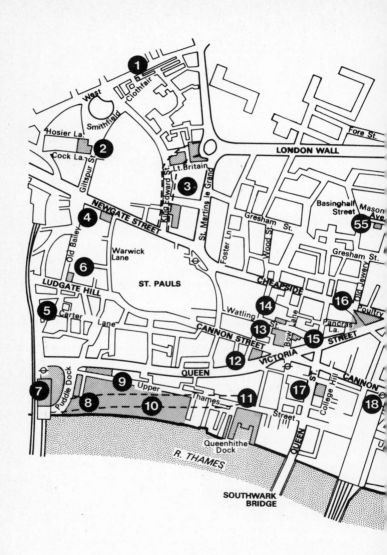

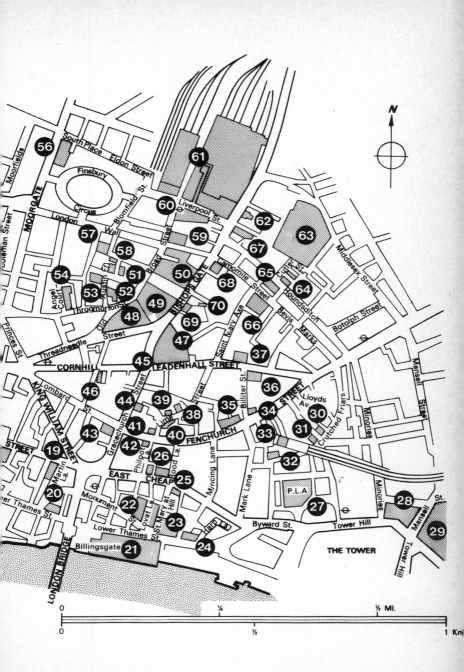

order to co-ordinate the likely large scale redevelopment.

In fact, there is no older part of the City which is not presently facing a barrage of proposals. One of the saddest losses will be several of the remaining areas of little courts, alleys and hidden corners, which give the City much of its character: the steep, cobbled lanes leading up from Billingsgate; Austin Friars and Copthall Court; Great St. Helens and Little Britain. No less than four recent schemes are crowded into the tiny Bow Lane Conservation Area, two of them major.

However, the City is said to be reconsidering its earlier proposal to drive a new widened road along Carter Lane. Similarly the earlier threat to the fine Leadenhall Market seems to have receded, although this western approach may be clipped off by the widening of Gracechurch St, and extensive redevelopment is proposed in narrow Lime St to the east.

1

1   Cloth Fair, the Rising Sun public house. Owned by St Bartholomew's Hospital, this pub has been closed and allowed to decay.
2   24–30 West Smithfield, 14–21 Hosier Lane and 21–30 Cock Lane. **P.** Offices.
A. Fitzroy Robinson and Partners.
D. Union International Co. of Smithfield.
3   Little Britain, Cross Keys Square, Cox's Court. City Corporation is buying up properties in and behind Little Britain at a cost of £3,600,000 for demolition, to make way for extension of London Wall through to King Edward's St. Interesting warehouse, pub and Georgian shopfront, opposite gardens of St Botolph's Without.

 3a   3b

3c

3d

5a

5a-b, Carter Lane

5b

3a, King Edward St; 3b, Cross Keys Court; 3c-d, Little Britain

5c, Broadway

4 3–5 Newgate St. **P.** Offices.
A. Richard Seifert. **D.** Sterling Land.
5 Carter Lane area. The City's long-standing proposal to drive a new road through the narrow streets south of St Paul's (along the line of Carter Lane) is now being re-considered. Development in this conservation area is therefore now likely to be piecemeal, and redevelopment may at last be expected on the bomb sites to the south of Ludgate Hill.

119

6

City

6 Corner of Ludgate Hill and Old Bailey. Impressive shop premises owned by the City Corporation. Recently vacated, future seems very uncertain.

7 Blackfriars station and adjoining site of a now disused cold store. **P.** New station, 131,000 sq ft offices (retaining place names in new facade). **A.** Richard Seifert. **D.** British Rail and Kings College Cambridge.

8 Mermaid Theatre. The theatre is moving to the Barbican Arts Centre, so its present site will be available for re-development. **P.** Offices. **A.** R. Seifert. **D.** Amalgamated Investments.

9 153–65 Queen Victoria St, including London Auction Mart. To be redeveloped as part of Faraday Building extension.

10 Area south of Upper Thames St. Has been cleared by the City Corporation for the new through route between Blackfriars and Upper Thames St. Various new buildings will stand here including the new City of London Boys school.

7

9

8

10

11   50–8 Upper Thames St and Queen
Hithe Dock, the last 'working' Thames-side
wharf in the City. **P.** 65,000 sq ft offices,
223 bedroom hotel. **A.** Hubbard Ford
and Partners. **D.** R. G. Lawrence.
12   Bounded by Bread St, Cannon St
and 90–100 Queen Victoria St (including
remains of blitzed St Mildred's Church).
P. 60,000 sq ft offices. **D.** Haslemere
Estates.
13   39–53 Cannon St, 19–26 Watling St,
5–9 Watling Court, 11–14 Bow Lane and
Salter's Court. This large scheme is in the
tiny Bow Lane Conservation Area and
contains many listed buildings. **P.** Offices,
trade centre, shops, pub, restaurant.
D. Worshipful Company of Salters and
Electricity Supply Nominees Ltd. The
proposal has been refused but is under
appeal to the DOE.

13a

13a, Cannon St; 13b, Bow Lane;
13c-d, Watling St

13b

13c

13d

14, Groveland Court

14 6–9 Bow Lane, 72–7 Watling St, 9–12 Bow Church Yard and 1–4 Groveland Court (conservation area including listed buildings). **P.** 47,000 sq ft offices and shops. **A.** C. H. Elsom Pack. **D.** Bow Lane Developments Ltd, a subsidiary of London Merchant Securities.

15 30–2 Watling St (in conservation area). **P.** 7-storey block offices. Application originally submitted by Land Investors Ltd. and refused. Similar application re-submitted under the name of Betjohn Properties. Demolition 1972.

16 Site bounded by Poultry, Bucklersbury, Pancras Lane, Sise Lane and Queen Victoria St. One of the most important sites in the City, overlooking Mansion House and Royal Exchange. **P.** 19-storey office tower block and piazza in front of Mansion House. **A.** William Holford (with Mies van de Rohe as consultant). **D.** Rugarth Investments.

17 Site bounded by 65–6 Queen St and 1–3 College Hill. **P.** Offices. **D.** Spire Investments.

18 80–4 Cannon St, Bush Lane House. **P.** 55,000 sq ft offices. **A.** Arup Associates. **D.** Trafalgar House.

16

16a

16a-b, Queen Victoria St

16b

21a, Billingsgate

21b, New Fresh Wharf

19 110–14 Cannon St, 22–5 Laurence Pounteney Lane, and 1–6 Martin Lane. **P.** Offices, shops, pub, flats (and Listed Building Demolition Consent for 17th-century 6 Martin Lane including Old Wine Shades). **D.** City of London Real Property. Demolition of Old Wine Shades stopped after public inquiry. Revised application in preparation.

20 131–7 Upper Thames St, 15 Arthur St including King William Street House. **P.** Offices. **D.** City of London Real Property.

21 Billingsgate Market (Sir Horace Jones, 1875) and New Fresh Wharf. **P.** New market building with 12-storey offices above and bridge across Lower Thames St (although market may move altogether). **A.** Richard Seifert. **D.** Billingsgate Market Authority.

22 Lovat Lane, Botolph Lane area. Likely to be extensively redeveloped following rebuilding of Billingsgate Market.

23 Corner of Lower Thames St, St Mary at Hill and 1–8 St Dunstan's Lane. J. B. Bunning's Coal Exchange, 1849, was demolished in November 1962 for urgent road widening, but nothing has been done with the site. **P.** Offices. **D.** Town and Commercial Developments.

24 Bounded by Lower Thames St, St Dunstan's Hill and Harp Lane. **P.** 63,000 sq ft offices and pub. **A.** Fitzroy and Robinson and Partners.

22a
22b

22a, Monument St; 22b, Lovat Lane

25, Eastcheap

26a
26b

25 Bounded by 30–40 Eastcheap, St Mary at Hill and 2–4 Idol Lane. **P.** Offices. **D.** City of London Real Property.
26 23–39 Eastcheap, 14–15 Philpot Lane and 10–13 Rood Lane. Interesting Victorian buildings, including Roumieu and Gough's Gothic fantasia in 33–5 Eastcheap, of which facade will be incorporated in new block. **P.** Offices, shops, car park. **D.** City of London Real Property.

26a, Philpot Lane; 26b, Eastcheap

28, Royal Mint St

27 PLA building. Being reconstructed internally to provide 168,000 sq ft offices. **D.** Amalgamated Investments.
28 Site bounded by Royal Mint St, The Minories, Tower Hill and Mansell St. **P.** Graduate business studies centre for City University and car parking for City Corporation.

124

City

29   Royal Mint (facing Tower Hill), by Johnson and Smirke 1808–11. D.O.E. plans huge office development on and behind.
30   5 Lloyd's Avenue. **P.** Offices. **A.** Gollins Melvin Ward. **D.** City of London Real Property.
31   Corner of Crutched Friars and Lloyd's Avenue. **P.** 22,000 sq ft offices. **D.** Haslemere Estates.
32   34–8 Crutched Friars and 2–3 New London St (London House). **P.** Offices, flats, shops, pub. **A.** C. H. Elsom and Partners. **D.** City of London Real Property.
33   Fenchurch St Station. Owing to listing of fine Victorian facade, office proposals are being reconsidered.
34   109–14 Fenchurch St and 17–18 Billiter St. **P.** Offices. **A.** Fitzroy Robinson.
35   120–4 Fenchurch St, Fen Court and Hogarth Court. **P.** Offices, restaurant. **A.** T. P. Bennett. **D.** Trafalgar House.
36   22–8 Billiter St and 42–9 Leadenhall St (including Africa House). **P.** Offices, restaurant, shops. **A.** Fitzroy Robinson. **D.** Trafalgar House.
37   96–103 Leadenhall St. **P.** Offices. **A.** Fitzroy Robinson. **D.** Trafalgar House.
38   8–11 Lime St and 2–14 Beehive Passage. **P.** Offices, shops. **D.** City of London Real Property.
39   12–13 Lime St. **P.** Offices, shops. **D.** London Indemnity and General Insurance.
40   27–30 Lime St (listed buildings, including Ship Inn). **P.** Road widening and redevelopment, for offices, shops, new pub. **Ap.** Truman Ltd. in association with The Guild or Fraternity of The Blessed Virgin Mary of the Mystery of Drapers of the City of London.

29

33

36a-b, Billiter St

36a

36b

City

41 Barclay's Bank on corner of Lime
St and Fenchurch St. **P.** To be re-
developed as part of Barclay's head-
quarters scheme on corner of Fenchurch
St and Gracechurch St. **D.** Lime Bank
Properties, a consortium of Barclay's,
City Corporation and City of London
Real Property.
42 5–12 Fenchurch St and 1 Philpot
Lane. **P.** Offices, shops. **D.** City of
London Real Property.
43 Corner of Lombard St and Grace-
church St (Credit Lyonnais). **P.** Offices.
A. Ley Colbeck and Partners. **D.** City
Offices.

41

46, Cornhill

44 78–82 Gracechurch St and 1, 4, 9,
and 12 Bull's Head Passage. **P.** Offices,
shops, pub. **D.** City of London Real
Property.
45 Buildings along Bishopsgate and
Gracechurch St are to be affected by
major road widening scheme between
Bishopsgate and London Bridge. Current
developments on these streets (e.g. 44
and 47) are to be set back in accordance
with new line of road, and remaining
buildings shoud be subject to redevelopment in the next few years. Leadenhall
Market, which it seemed at one time
might be directly affected by the scheme,
is now to stay – although the character of
its approaches is being eroded by extensive piecemeal redevelopment.
46 39 Cornhill, 4 Castle Court (excluding the George and Vulture and Simpson's
Tavern). **P.** Offices. **A.** Richard Seifert.
D. Union Discount Co. This scheme was
turned down after a public inquiry but
appeal to the Minister has still to be heard.
47 2–26 Bishopsgate, 148–59 Leadenhall St. This important corner site includes
Norman Shaw's Barings Bank building
(1881) and the french-style Banque
Belge. **P.** £60 million scheme to include
banking halls and office tower block.
A. Gollins Melvin Ward. **D.** Barings,
Banque and Anthony Gibbs. Permission
has been given to pull down the listed
Barings Bank building.

47, Barings Bank

48   1–17 Old Broad St (including Philip Hardwick's City Club, 1831) and 41–53 Threadneedle St. Part of the huge scheme centred on Richard Seifert's 600-ft headquarters for the National Westminster Bank (see 49). Permission for the demolition of the City Club was granted some years ago, although in 1964 the Ministry made a preservation order on Gibson's National Provincial Bank in Bishopsgate, which was scheduled for demolition under the same scheme. Several attempts have since been made to get the City Club similarly preserved, by a comparatively small modification of Seifert's scheme, but all have failed. This refusal has been made somewhat ironic by the decision of Peter Walker in 1972 to forbid the demolition of Mewes and Davies' National Westminster Bank at 51–3 Threadneedle St which has involved expensive alterations not only to Seifert's plans, but also to the City Corporation's plan for a system of first-floor elevated pedestrian ways.

49   Site between Old Broad St and Bishopsgate. London's tallest tower block, 600 ft headquarters of the National Westminster Bank, is being built. **A.** Richard Seifert. **D.** National Westminster Bank.

48a
48b

48a, City Club (to go); 48b, Old Broad St (to go); 48c, National Westminster Bank (to stay); 48d, Gibson's Bank (to stay)

48c

48d

51

52

City

50 Site bounded by Old Broad St, Wormwood St and Bishopsgate (including Union Court and Peahen Court). **P.** 30-storey office tower block. **A.** Richard Seifert and Ley Colbeck and Partners. **D.** Bishopsgate Developments (an associate of Barclay Hambro Property).
51 8–12 Austin Friars. **P.** 100,000 sq ft offices. **A.** Richard Seifert. **D.** Amalgamated Investments.
52 2–6 Austin Friars. City of London Real Property has plans for major office redevelopment.

53

53 22–3 Austin Friars. **P.** Offices. **D.** Thomas Saunders.
54 2–8 Angel Court, 1–2 Copthall Buildings, 1–5 and 11–18 Copthall Court, 1–4 Copthall Chambers and 30–2 Throgmorton St. **P.** Offices, flats, bank, shops. **A.** Fitzroy Robinson. **D.** Clothworkers' Company.

54, Copthall Court

City

55 1 Mason's Avenue (Ye Olde Doctor Butler's Head). The Governors of Christ's Hospital have applied for a Listed Building Demolition Consent.

56 Bounded by Moorgate, South Place and South Place Mews. **P.** 86,000 sq ft offices, shops and car parking (Finsbury Pavement House). **A.** Richard Seifert. **D.** Stock Conversion.

57 3–7 Throgmorton Avenue and 23–5 Great Winchester St. **P.** Offices. **D.** Morgan Grenfell Holdings and Worshipful Company of Carpenters.

58 19 Great Winchester St. **P.** Offices. **D.** Amalgamated Investments.

59 Broad Street House. **P.** 125,000 sq ft offices over 2 floors shops. **A.** Ley Colbeck and Partners. **D.** Trafalgar House.

60 17–34 Liverpool St Arcade. Proposals for redevelopment appear to be in abeyance.

57, 58, Great Winchester St

54, Angel Court

55

59

City

61 Liverpool St and Broad St Stations.
Redevelopment has been discussed. The
Baltic Exchange may build their proposed
£100 million world shipping centre here.
In 1972 they were granted a 500,000 sq
ft Office Development Permit for this, and
their architect Richard Seifert has had
discussions with British Rail (see also
63 below).

61a, Liverpool St Station

61b-c, Broad St Station

62

62 162–4 Bishopsgate, Gothic Fire
Station by George Vulliamy 1885, now
disused (owned by GLC). Redevelopment
seems likely, possibly with adjoining
buildings.

City

63 Cutler St Warehouses, covering $4\frac{1}{2}$-acres, built between 1770 and 1820 for the East India Company. Owners PLA have recently been trying to sell them for possible redevelopment, although several of the buildings (including 18th-century houses) are listed, which might make this a complicated procedure. Possible site for new shipping centre for Baltic Exchange, but listing difficulties would seem to make Liverpool St Station a more likely site (see 61 above).
64 2–8 Cutler St, 2–8 Clothier St, and 115–16 Houndsditch. **P.** Offices, shops. **D.** Worshipful Company of Cutlers.
65 47–56 Houndsditch, 66–70 St Mary Axe and 10–11 Goring St. **P.** Offices. **D.** Great Universal Stores.
66 Site bounded by St Mary Axe, Bevis Marks and Bury Court. **P.** 220,000 sq ft offices. **D.** Haslemere Estates.
67 142–50 Bishopsgate and 2–11 Devonshire Row. **P.** Offices, shops. **D.** Star Great Britain.
68 88–102 Bishopsgate, 1–11 Camomile St, 1–11 Wrestlers Court, Norgrove Buildings and Clark's Place. **P.** 132,500 sq ft offices and shops. **A.** Fitzroy Robinson. **D.** J. L. P. Investments.

63

69, Bishopsgate

70

69 42–50 Bishopsgate and 36–8 Great St Helen's. **P.** Offices, shops, bank. **D.** Skinners' Company.
70 34 and 35 Great St Helen's. **P.** Offices. **D.** Trafalgar House.

Late entries (not on map)
71 20–40 Eastcheap. Redevelopment
has been discussed. MEPC are planning a
70,000 sq ft office and bank development
somewhere in Eastcheap, maybe here.
72 Chiswell St. Whitbread's Brewery.
6½-acre jumble of 18th and 19th century
buildings, including Porter Tun Room,
with clear span timber-trussed roof second
only to Westminster Hall. Whitbread's in
alliance with Trafalgar House have plans
for 630,000 sq ft offices (retaining listed
buildings). So far, however, the site is
still zoned by the GLC for industrial use
only. **A.** Fitzroy Robinson.

13. Southwark

New Southwark

The largest-scale redevelopment planned anywhere in London is
just beginning along almost a mile of the Thames in north Southwark.
This whole area is a mass of 19th-century narrow lanes and canyons,
cutting through the great mid-Victorian warehouses, docks and
factories which stretch from Blackfriars down to Tower Bridge.
Here and there are fragments of earlier ages — 17th- and
18th-century houses on Bankside around Christopher Wren's home
and the much restored Anchor Inn.

   Now almost all of this is to be swept away (including the well-
known view of the docks above Tower Bridge) to make way for
some of the most massive office developments in London. At the
western end on Kings Reach, an office, flat and hotel complex by
Richard Seifert was already beginning to rise at the end of 1972.
Next to Bankside power station, a site was being cleared for Lloyd's
Bank's huge new computer centre, isolating Wren's house (listed).
To the east, the tower blocks are already rising around London
Bridge Station, the oldest in London, the front of which was
demolished in 1972. Between here and the river lies the site of
Renslade's vast Hay's Wharf scheme, the largest of all. Renslade
have made some concessions to placate the conservationists and
have asked Denys Lasdun to design the stretch in front of Southwark
Cathedral. A garden here will open up views of the cathedral from
the river for the first time in over a hundred years. The 14th-century
rose-window from Winchester Palace, now bricked into a warehouse
wall, is to remain as a ruin in the garden. Hibernia Chambers by
London Bridge is to be done up.

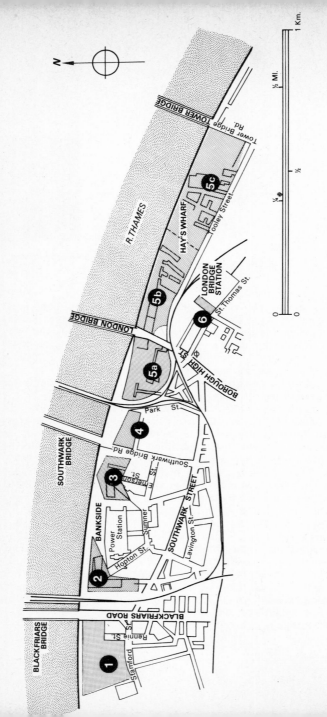

N

R. THAMES

TOWER BRIDGE

Tower Bridge Rd.

5c

HAY'S WHARF

Pooley Street

5b

LONDON BRIDGE

LONDON
BRIDGE
STATION

6

St. Thomas St.

5a

BOROUGH HIGH ST.

SOUTHWARK
BRIDGE

Park St.

4

Southwark Bridge Rd

3

Emerson St.

BANKSIDE

Power
Station

Sumner St.

SOUTHWARK STREET

Lavington St.

2

Hopton St.

BLACKFRIARS
BRIDGE

BLACKFRIARS ROAD

Rennie St.

Stamford St.

1

0   ¼   ½   1 Km.

0   ¼   ½ Ml.

5a

5b

1 Site on the Thames west of Blackfriar's Bridge, by Broadwall, Stampford St and Rennie St. Formerly wharves and warehouses, now the King's Reach scheme. **P.** 350,000 sq ft offices, 750 room hotel (rising to 12 storeys) 200 flats, shops, restaurant, riverside walk. **A.** Richard Seifert. **D.** A consortium including IPC, Sainsburys and Spanish Melia Hotel group.

5a-c, Hay's Wharf

5c

2 Site to the east of Blackfriars Bridge, extending from Southwark St up Hopton St and along Bankside. Formerly goods station. **P.** 564,000 sq ft building, for offices and Lloyd's Bank computer centre. Also 140 riverside flats and open space. **A.** Fitzroy Robinson **D.** Edger Investments.

3 Site behind Christopher Wren's house east of Bankside Power Station, including Skin Market Place, Emerson St, Bear Gardens etc. Presently wharves and warehouses. Nature of redevelopment has not yet been established, but may include Sam Wanamaker's plans for a new Globe Theatre.

4 Site fronting river between Southwark Bridge and Cannon St Railway Bridge. **P.** 200,000 sq ft offices, 150 flats, possibly theatre. **A.** T. P. Bennett. **D.** John Laing.

5 The Hay's Wharf site. $38\frac{1}{2}$-acres along the river between Clink St and Tower Bridge. Most of area presently covered by Victorian dock and warehouse buildings stretching down Tooley St. It is to be developed in three sections:

Southwark

5d, Hibernia Wharf

a. Hibernia Wharf between railway bridge and London Bridge. Original proposal by Renslade (jointly owned by Michael Rivkin and Amalgamated Investments) for 379,000 sq ft offices in blocks up to 23-storeys, altered to include open space with trees between Southwark Cathedral and the Thames and has been accepted.
b. Western half of Tooley St behind the City of London Corporation tower block overlooking New London Bridge. Original proposal by St Martin's Property Corporation was for 939,000 sq ft offices in blocks up to 35-storeys high with hotel on Hay's Dock.
c. 23-acres between Battle Bridge Lane and Tower Bridge. Original proposal by Renslade was for 857,000 sq ft offices in blocks up to 32-storeys and 480 flats in five 'coffin shaped' blocks up to 13-storeys.

6 London Bridge Station. **P.** 200,000 sq ft offices with re-construction of parts of station. **D.** Peachey Property Corporation in conjunction with British Rail.

Late entry, not on map
7 Site east of Waterloo Bridge, directly behind Denys Lasdun's new National Theatre. **P.** 380-ft hotel. **A.** Derek Stephenson. **D.** Heron Corp. for Holiday Inns.

6

14. Periphery

It is beyond the province of this book to deal in any detail with the vast reaches of London which lie outside our immediate central area, although there is scarcely a district which is not undergoing major change.

1. Dockland

Perhaps the greatest changes which face any part of London in the coming years are those which will take place in dockland. Since the closure of the major docks on the higher reaches of the river in the late sixties and early seventies, more than 5,000 acres of wharves, docks, warehouses, dockside industry and housing have become available for redevelopment — an area the size of the City of Westminster. This daunting prospect of the need to redevelop on a scale which no major city has ever had to face before, was in 1971 made the subject of a £500,000 government-sponsored study.

The first dock on which redevelopment has already begun, St Katharine's, is untypical; firstly in that, like the Southwark waterfront, it is strategically placed near to the City, secondly in that it contains buildings considered to be of sufficient architectural and historical merit to justify expensive conversion and conservation of some of Telford and Hardwick's warehouses as part of the scheme. The first phase of the World Trade Centre, already begun, is designed by Andrew Renton for developers Taylor Woodrow; a further 1,100,000 sq ft of trading floors are due in phase two.

St Katharine's Dock

Periphery

2. 19th-century housing
Some of the most characteristic London townscapes are to be found
in the 19th-century two-storey brick terraces with their plaster
cornices which are now being replaced by the tower blocks of
council housing schemes across hundreds of acres of Camden,
Kentish Town, Kilburn, Lisson Grove, Clapham, Wandsworth,
Brixton, Camberwell, Deptford, New Cross, the East End and almost
every district of comparable character.

In the other parts of the East End, many once-fashionable 18th-
and early 19th-century houses have also been razed, as in the
squares of Stepney. Ironically, Arbor Square (1803), presently
threatened, is like areas in Lambeth and Islington which have
recently become fashionable.

Terraces in Caledonian Road, Islington, being demolished for warehousing by David Canaan Properties. These were listed in 1972, but planning consent had already been granted.

Acres of Kentish Town razed for re-development.

3. Large Victorian houses
Speculators have recently been moving in on the 19th-century,
large, detached houses, which gave character to so many of the
outlying parts of London. Although usually ideal for conversion into
flats, these houses offer perfect sites for high-density residential
development. Two areas where such developments have recently
aroused notable local concern are Gloucester Avenue in Camden
Town, and Beulah Hill and Crystal Palace Park Rd, rising up
Sydenham Hill in Norwood. The Regency Montpelier House in
Kentish Town also faces redevelopment by Camden.

6, 8 and 10 Gloucester Avenue were demolished in 1972 (4 above to follow). Hills Structures and Foundations is replacing them with 5 blocks of 6-storey luxury flats designed by Ronald Salmon. GLC Historic Buildings department and Victorian Society both campaigned against demolition in 1970, but the proposal had come to their notice too late for any effective action to be taken.

4. Churches

Often conspicuous local landmarks, many churches are threatened with redundancy. Once a church is utenable, its future is discussed by a succession of responsible bodies, culminating in the Advisory Board for Redundant Churches. This complex process may take between one and three years, during which time alternative uses are considered. Once the building is declared officially redundant, it is available for lease, gift or sale, and may be redeveloped. If it is considered exceptional, the Minister may assume responsibility.

Proposals for conversion, or alternative use, should be put to The Council for Places of Worship, 83 London Wall, E.C.2. Also the Church Commissioners, 1 Millbank, S.W.1, have the complete list of already redundant churches.

These are some examples of London churches which are to be demolished, or whose future is uncertain.

Christ Church, Highbury Grove, Islington   St Stephen, Rosslyn Hill

a

d

b

a, St Peter, Davona Rd, Islington; b, St
Michael, Shoreditch; c, St Columbia,
Shoreditch; d, St Peter, Elgin Avenue;
e, All Saints, Hackney; f, St James,

c

e

f

h

i

*Islington; g, St Saviour, Maida Vale;
h, Holy Trinity, Islington; i, St Paul,
Hammersmith; j, St Augustine,
Shoreditch*

g

j

Periphery

5. Other buildings

The erosion of particularly notable buildings outside central London has slowed recently, with the awakening of conservationist feeling. Upton House, Newham, was lost, but the Granada, Tooting, the Gothic castellated Waterworks Pumping Station in Stoke Newington and Teulon's almshouses in Penge have all been saved (and in the last instance, rehabilitated).

Among the buildings whose future is threatened, or which have recently been demolished are the following:

Lyric Theatre, Hammersmith. Demolished in 8-acre scheme north of King St for 415,000 sq ft offices and shops, parking for 1,000 cars, entertainment centre and 200 council flats. **A.** Richard Seifert, for St Martin's Property Corporation and Hammersmith.

Granville Theatre, Fulham. Demolished by Romulus for offices and showrooms in 1972. This 1890 theatre escaped listing because DOE inspectors did not see fine interior, but incident led to a thorough investigation of all London theatres, and several were added to list.

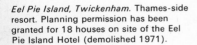

Eel Pie Island, Twickenham. Thames-side resort. Planning permission has been granted for 18 houses on site of the Eel Pie Island Hotel (demolished 1971).

Agricultural Hall, Islington. A minor Olympia, built in 1861–2. Its 150-ft iron span covers a hall 384 ft by 217 ft. Developer R. G. Lawrence wishes to demolish, and Islington are amenable, although local groups would like preservation for sports facilities.

Periphery

Three Mills, Bromley-le-Bow. One of the finest surviving early-Victorian industrial complexes including the Clock and House tide-mills and a distillery. Bass Charrington Vintners wish to redevelop the whole area for their new South of England bottling and storage centre. The Clock Mill is to be converted, but an application for demolition consent has been made on the House Mill, listed Grade One.

Three Mills

Camden Passage Islington (mid-18th-century). Proposal for demolition of 47–9, with balcony and original shop-front, to make way for shopping arcade and maisonettes.
Angel, Islington. The controversial GLC road-widening scheme here will involve demolition of mid-19th-century Philharmonic Hall.

Alexandra Palace, Muswell Hill (1875). In 1978 the users of this 'fun-palace' (BBC, Hornsey College of Art and a car auction firm) are moving out. In 1972 development suggestions were invited although there is strong local feeling for retaining the building.

Alexandra Palace

Teulon's almshouses, Penge (rehabilitated)

Developers

The technique of speculative development is something in which Britain has led the world. Traditionally an office building was commissioned by the company which was going to occupy it. This meant that the architect could work to a specific brief, and that expense and care could be lavished on the design.

Today the vast majority of offices are built on speculation. The prime consideration is to produce the maximum square footage of space, to the maximum plot ratio, at the cheapest possible cost.

Over the past forty years, property development has thus grown into a highly complex — and of course highly lucrative — game, in which five groups of people are involved. Firstly there are the developers themselves. Secondly there are the estate agents, who help them to look out for and acquire the necessary sites (and of course to help them let the property when it is complete). Thirdly there are the architects, who are as much experts in planning procedure as they are designers. Fourth there are the local authority planners, with whom any scheme has to be agreed. Fifth there are the financial backers for the whole operation, who may be insurance companies, banks or building contractors.

Among the main companies presently involved in central London redevelopment (with conservative estimates of assets as of 1972) are:
Land Securities (£800 million)
Star (Great Britain) (£400 million)
MEPC (£300 million)
Trafalgar House (£230 million)
Capital and Counties (£170 million)
Town and City (£100 million)
Stock Conversion (£80 million)
Amalgamated Investments (£64 million)
London Merchant Securities (£60 million)
Haslemere Estates (£53 million)

Some idea of the astonishing growth of the property boom in the past twelve years may be gained from the fact that when Charles Clore, Jack Cotton and Walter Flack amalgamated their interests in 1960 to form City Centre, it was by far the largest property company in the world, with total assets of just over £60 million.

Gabriel Harrison   *Leslie Marler*

Amalgamated Investments and Property Co Ltd, 9–10 Grafton St, W.1. (499–0432) Chairman and Managing Director: Gabriel Harrison. One of the fastest growing companies in recent years. Gabriel Harrison was b. Kilburn in 1921, and began building houses in Ruislip after 1945. His first big development in central London was Regina House (1959), a nine-storey block at the corner of the Edgware and Marylebone Rds. In 1960 he was bought out by Jack Cotton, and with the proceeds formed Amalgamated in 1961. One of his biggest coups has been arrangement with U.K. Provident to develop properties in their ownership. In recent years he has employed most of the big developers' architects, and describes himself as Seifert's biggest client at the moment. (e.g. Whittington House in Alfred Place). The developments of which he is proudest are the internal conversion of the PLA building, and a new block by Michael Lyell between Curzon St and Stanhope Gate, which involved the retention of two Georgian facades. He is keen to placate preservationist feeling. He recently bought the 18th-century Grand Junction Co. (which owns Paddington Basin and surrounding land). Among his current schemes are the redevelopment of Waring and Gillow, Windsor House and the huge Hays Wharf scheme (in association with his onetime employee Michael Rivkin). Lives in a Nash house in Regents Park.
Projects: **4** 26, **5** 32, **7** 11, **7** 12, **7** 14, **7** 20, **8** 3, **9** 3, **9** 5, **11** 8, **11** 8a, **12** 27, **12** 51, **12** 58, **13** 5.
Amalgamated Securities Ltd, 7 Albemarle St, W.1. (499–5018)
Chairman: Jack Morrison. Deputy-Chairman and Managing Director:
Michael Morrison
Project: **7** 15.
Bovis Ltd, Liscartan House, 127 Sloane St, SW1 (730–5155).
Chairman: Harry Vincent. Mainly engaged in construction.
Project: **2** 30.
Bow Lane Developments Ltd, 6 Charterhouse Square, EC1 (253–5581).
A jointly-owned subsidiary of the Church Commissioners and London
Merchant Securities.
British Land Co Ltd, 53 Grosvenor St, W1 (499–9114) Chairman and
Managing Director: John Ritblat.
Project: **7** 31.

Developers

Capital and Counties Property Co Ltd, 40 Broadway, SW1 (930–7501)
Hon. President: *Leslie Marler*. Chairman: Sir Richard Thompson Bt. MP.
Joint-Managing Director: D. R. G. Marler. Many of their developments have
been in the Knightsbridge area, in conjunction with the Cadogan Estate,
including the Pantechnicon scheme off Motcomb St, multi-storey car park in
Pavilion Rd and the Seifert-designed Park Tower hotel (on Woollands site).
Other recent London developments: Hanover Square (east side), Field House,
Breams Buildings.
Projects: **2** 11, **7** 22, **8** 7, **11** 9.

City Side and Ariel Developments Ltd, 228 Fulham Rd, SW10 (352–3707).
Directors: Anthony Apponyi, Martin Radford
Project: **1** 7.

City of London Real Property Co Ltd, Vincula House, Tower Place, EC3
(623–3123). The oldest and once the largest property company, formed in
1964. Taken over in 1969 for £160 million by Land Securities.
Projects: see under Land Securities.

Compass Securities, 9 Hill St, W1 (629–1355). A subsidiary of Guardian
Royal Exchange Assurance Ltd.
Projects: **7** 7, **11** 1, **11** 12.

Country and New Towns Properties Ltd, 425 Strand, WC2 (240–1181).
Owns large block of property on north side of the Strand, including Civil
Service Stores. Effectively controlled by Sir Nicholas Cayzer's British
Commonwealth and Shipping Co.
Project: **9** 29.

Edger Investments, 115 Park St, W1 (499–1614) Chairman and Managing
Director: Gerald A. Glover. Another director is Sir Edwin McAlpine. Glover,
McAlpine and Lord Cadogan laid plans in the early sixties for extensive
development on the Cadogan Estate, including a 26-storey block on Pont St,
but the only major project completed was the Carlton Tower Hotel. Glover
and McAlpine were also involved in the development of St Alphage House on
Route II.
Projects: **2** 22, **13** 2.

Green Garden Investment Ltd.
Director: Robin Spiro
Project: **4** 18.

Haslemere Estates, 4 Carlos Place, W1 (629–1105) Chairman: F. E. Cleary.
Managing Director: D. M. Pickford. Specialists in modernisation and
restoration of existing buildings for prestige offices, e.g. 18th-century 46
Berkeley Square. Also have new developments in the City and Covent Garden.
Projects: **9** 8, **9** 27, **12** 12, **12** 31, **12** 66.

Octavia Hill Housing Trust, 89 Princedale Rd, W11 (727–5976).
Chairman: R. Ouvry. Director:
Mainly engaged in housing developments in N.W. Kensington.
Projects: **1** 6, **1** 8.

Developers

Land Securities Investment Trust Ltd, Devonshire House, Piccadilly W1 (493–4433). Chairman: Lord Samuel of Wych Cross. By far the largest of the property companies: among companies it has taken over are Ravenseft (specialising in provincial shopping centres) and Westminster Trust Holdings, developers of New Scotland Yard in Victoria St, the Gorringes site and the Elephant and Castle Centre.

Harold Samuel, b. 1912, son of founder of H. Samuel watch company. Educ. Mill Hill. In 1944 bought control of Land Securities, a tiny property company owning three houses in Kensington Court. At the end of the War he began buying large blocks of flats which had been requisitioned for wartime use as offices, by judicious juggling of bank loans and mortgages. By the mid-fifties he was emerging as the first well-known property speculator, but the

F. E. Cleary

Lord Samuel

failure of his much-publicised bid to take over the Savoy Group led him to retreat from the limelight. In 1963 became first property developer to be knighted. In 1968 Samuel bought out his old rival Charles Clore, with a £64 million bid for City Centre. In 1969 he outbid MEPC and Trafalgar House in a £160 million takeover of the giant City of London Real Property Co., with its 104 valuable office blocks in the City. In 1971 he gave £250,000 to the Chequers Fund. In 1972 he was awarded a Barony. Brother-in-law of Maxwell Joseph. Lives in Avenue Rd. and has a farm in Sussex.
Projects: **5** 11, **5** 24, **7** 19, **8** 4, **12** 19, **12** 20, **12** 25, **12** 26, **12** 30, **12** 32, **12** 38, **12** 41, **12** 42, **12** 44, **12** 52.

London Merchant Securities, 100 George St, W1 (935–3555). Chairman: Sir Max Rayne.

Rayne was b. 1918, son of Polish immigrant in rag trade. Began in property 1947. His first big development was in 1952 on an island block behind Selfridge's (now 3M House), on which he made a profit of £850,000. Rayne's style, established early, was to work through contacts with the big landowners. In 1955 he initiated the Church Commissioners into the development potential of their Paddington Estate; one result was the central tower-block on Eastbourne Terrace. There followed highly profitable associations with Eton College for the development of their Swiss Cottage estate (producing the series of tower-blocks looking down on Primrose Hill); and the Portman Estate, which has produced many mutually profitable developments in the area around Baker St. In 1960 set up London Merchant Securities. In 1965 married Lady Jane Vane-Tempest-Stuart. Lives in West Heath Rd, Hampstead; and was knighted in 1972.
Projects: **4** 9, **4** 10, **4** 12, **4** 13, **10** 9, **12** 14.

Lyon Group, 258 Grays Inn Rd, WC1 (837–0751).
Chairman and Managing Director: Ronald Lyon. This group is concerned with big development on Calthorpe estate. Also involved in new National Exhibition Centre scheme at Northolt (for which £10 million grant is forthcoming from GLC), and has holdings in redevelopment of Olympia and Earls Court.
Projects: **1** 28, **2** 24, **10** 16.

Metropolitan Estate and Property Corporation, 113 Park Lane, W1 (629–9022). Chairman: Sir Henry Johnson. Managing Director: Peter Anker. In recent years MEPC has become one of the most active property companies in London, particularly through its associations with Reed-IPC and Grosvenor Estate. Backed by Eagle Star.
Projects: **5** 36, **5** 37, **6** 22, **6** 24, **6** 25, **7** 6, **9** 10, **9** 12, **9** 14, **11** 19.

Peachey Property Corporation, Park West, Edgware Rd, W2 (262–0161). Chairman and Managing Director: E. M. Miller.
Project: **13** 6.

Renslade Investments. Formed in 1970 by Gabriel Harrison's Amalgamated Investments and Michael Rivkin to redevelop the Hays Wharf site, the largest redevelopment scheme in London. Rivkin, a flamboyant 7-footer, runs Argyll Securities, and is generally regarded as the master-mind of the vast Hays Wharf project.
Project: **53** 5.

Romulus Investments Ltd, Lodge House, Beaufort St, SW1 (352–1542). Chairman and Managing Director: P. Woolf. Presently redeveloping the old Granville Theatre in Fulham, and possibly 17th-century Sandford Manor.
Projects: **2** 32, **14** 5.

Rugarth Property Management Co. Ltd, 37a Walbrook, EC4 (626–9236). Chairman: Peter Palumbo. Their main project is the late Rudolph Palumbo's long-dreamed-of prestige tower-block in the City ('Palumbo Plaza').
Project: **12** 16.

Samuel Properties 197 Knightsbridge, SW7 (584–3331). Chairman: Viscount Bearsted. Managing Director: Sidney Cowan.
Project: **3** 5.

Sir Max Rayne

Peter Anker

Star (Great Britain) Holdings Ltd, 16 Grosvenor St W1 (499–0444).
Chairman: Sir Brian Mountain. Chief Executive: David Llewellyn. The company
was formed in 1959 and was built up in the sixties backed by Eagle Star
Insurance Co. Once involved in huge scheme for redevelopment of Victoria
Station. Owners of New London Theatre, Drury Lane.
Projects: **5** 19, **12** 67.

Sterling Guarantee Trust Ltd, 10 Babmaes St, SW1 (930–8225).
Chairman: Geoffrey Sterling. Presently involved in the huge schemes for Earls
Court, Olympia and the Gamages site in High Holborn.
Projects: **1** 28, **2** 24, **11** 4.

Stock Conversion and Investment Trust, 130 Jermyn St, SW1 (839–7361).
Chairman: Robert Clark. Directors include Joe Levy, majority shareholder.
Levy specialises in 'lease collection', as in his spectacular coup over Euston
Centre (1956–64). He was b. 1906 in Acton, son of a bookmaker. Educ.
Emmanuel School. Joined famous pre-war estate agent Jackie Phillips (later
D. E. and J. Levy). As a wartime fireman, Levy's knowledge of bomb-
damaged sites gave him a head start in post-war property market. Clark and
Levy bought Stock Coversion in 1951, and first came to public notice with
unveiling of huge Euston Centre scheme in 1964.

Joe Levy and Robert Clark

Barry East

In 1967, Levy unveiled his second major coup, the Trocadero site. Other major recent operations have been in Euston Road and Kings Cross. Properties 'held for development' include Palace Theatre, Camden Theatre, and several in Covent Garden. Levy lives in Grosvenor Sq, and has a villa in Cap D'Antibes.

Projects: **1** 1, **4** 17, **5** 26, **5** 29, **6** 1, **7** 34, **9** 4, **10** 12, **10** 13, **10** 15, **12** 56.

Town and City Properties Ltd, 4 Carlton Gardens, SW1 (839–5611). Chairman: Barry East, b. N.W. London 1915. Former estate agent. Vice-President of Essex Cricket Club, and lives in St John's Wood. Made reputation from late fifties onwards as developer of shopping precincts. Active in Europe. Other major developments have included big schemes on four London stations. Major current involvements include Earls Court and Olympia, Gamages, and around Cambridge Circus. Many of Town and City's schemes have been backed by the Prudential Assurance Co.

Projects: **2** 24, **5** 31, 10 4, **11** 4.

Trafalgar House Ltd, Cleveland House, St James's Square, SW1 (930–9501). Chairman: Nigel Broackes. Managing Director: Victor Matthews. Broackes was b. 1934, son of Yorkshire solicitor. Educ. Stowe. First development on corner of Half Moon St, Piccadilly. In 1962 association with Commercial Union led to setting up of Trafalgar House. First major coup was Cleveland House on St James's Sq. In 1968 Trafalgar bought Trollope and Colls, the building and demolition firm, for which Broackes's partner Victor Matthews had previously worked as a foreman. Broackes's chief architect since 1958 has been Robert Chapman of Chapman Taylor (see Architects).

Projects: **2** 10, **6** 11, **6** 16, **12** 18, **12** 35, **12** 36, **12** 59, **12** 70, **12** 71, **12** 37.

Trust Houses Forte, 166 High Holborn, WC1 (836–1213). This giant hotel group is engaged in two large redevelopments, the Waldorf extension in Covent Garden, and the Criterion site in Piccadilly (although this ran into more trouble than either of the other two 1972 Piccadilly Circus schemes).

Projects: **5** 25, **2** 19, **9** 21.

Developers

University of London, Senate House, Malet St, WC1 (636–8000). In the view of conservationists, London University has probably been the most destructive developer in London since the War. Woburn Square is the third of the original Bloomsbury squares to be demolished for University extensions. Imperial College has caused great controversy over the past fifteen years with its forays in and around Queens Gate, Kensington. In the Strand, the new concrete blocks of Kings College have encroached remorselessly on several groups of remarkable old buildings (see under separate headings in main text). Principal of London University since 1948 has been Sir Douglas Logan (b. 1910) who has defended these ravages in the name of the necessities of learning.

National Car Parks Ltd, 14 Bishops Bridge Rd, W2 (723–3400). This private company plays an important part in the history of many developments. Between demolition and reconstruction (which may be a period of several years) NCP rent many sites for car parks. At present they operate 178 car parks in London, including some purpose-built multi-storey parks, with a total capacity of well over 40,000 cars. At a conservatively-averaged income of £1 a day per car space, this produces a total of at least a quarter of a million pounds a week, or £12 million a year, (minus rent and in most cases minimal operating costs). NCP also have twice as many car parks in other parts of Britain.

Architects

One of the features of the post-War development boom has been the emergence of a handful of 'developer's architects'. Although their names are by and large little known to the public, these men are responsible for the vast majority of London's big new redevelopment schemes. Their firms have built their reputations above all on their skill in using planning legislation to its best advantage, and their ability to produce buildings as quickly and economically as possible.

Occasionally, in instances where prestige or well-known locations are involved, a developer will also employ some distinguished name as 'consultant' – e.g. Sir Basil Spence, Lord Holford, Mies van der Rohe.

Architects

T. P. Bennett, 246 High Holborn, WC1 (405–9277). b. 1887. Designs include BOAC Air Terminal and Royal Lancaster Hotel, Bayswater.
Projects: **4** 14, **6** 4, **6** 17, **8** 4, **11** 7, **12** 35, **13** 4.

Sir John Burnet Tait and Partners, 10 Bedford Square, WC1 (580–3826). Sir John Burnet died in thirties. Present head of firm Gordon Tait. Recent designs include series of blocks along north side of Victoria Street flanking Westminster City Hall, and West London Air Terminal.
Projects: **2** 33, **4** 11, **4** 27, **5** 24, **10** 23.

Chapman, Taylor, 145 Kensington Church St, W8 (229–9851). Long association with Nigel Broackes's Trafalgar House. Notable schemes include Trafalgar House's headquarters Cleveland House, Bristol Hotel Piccadilly, and Scotland Yard complex in Victoria St. Also recently engaged by Grosvenor Estate to prepare its Strategy for Mayfair and Belgravia, and Crown Estates to undertake development of the vast Bessborough Gardens scheme.
Projects: **2** 10, **4** 28, **4** 33, **6** 5, **6** 11, **7** 3, **7** 16, **7** 24, **7** 31, **7** 35, **10** 15.

Cubitt, Nichols, 6 Bolton St, W1 (499–7517). Mainly engaged on re-development of Sutton Settled Estates properties in Soho and Mayfair.
Projects: **5** 6, **5** 7, **5** 8, **5** 9, **6** 7.

C. H. Elsom, Pack, Roberts and Partners, 21 Douglas St, SW1 (834–4411). b. West Ham 1912, son of Russian-Jewish tailor. At 20 won competition for Welwyn Garden City Town Hall. Has been associated with Max Rayne since 1947 and worked on many of his major projects (including Eastbourne Terrace, for which he won a Civic Trust award). The design of which he is proudest is the rehabilitation and reconstruction of 17th-century Schomberg House in Pall Mall. His major current projects include several for London Merchant Securities around Baker St, and a series of huge developments in Victoria St (including the stepped blocks and piazza in front of Westminster Cathedral).
Projects: **4** 6, **4** 9, **4** 10, **4** 12, **4** 13, **5** 19, **7** 9, **7** 10, **7** 11, **7** 15, **7** 23, **12** 14, **12** 32.

C. H. Elsom's Eastbourne Terrace

Chapman Taylor's Bristol Hotel

Architects

Fitzroy Robinson

Fitzroy Robinson's Stock Exchange

Fitzroy Robinson and Partners, 3 Grays Inn Rd, WC1 (405–0853). Herbert Fitzroy Robinson is one of the longer-established architects. His buildings include the London Press Exchange, Rothschild's Bank, and the Language Tuition Centre. Also involved with other architects in the new Stock Exchange building.

Projects: **5** 26, **7** 19, **12** 2, **12** 24, **12** 34, **12** 36, **12** 37, **12** 54, **12** 68, **13** 2.

Gollins, Melvin, Ward and Partners, 18 Manchester Square, W1 (486–6655). Designs include Castrol House in Marylebone Rd, Commercial Union tower in City. Present projects include Royal Opera House extension, and huge Barings Bank scheme.

Projects: **2** 17, **6** 14, **7** 7, **9** 17, **12** 30, **12** 47.

Gollins Melvin Ward's Commercial Union

Sidney Kaye (see overleaf)

Architects

Frederick Gibberd and Partners, 8 Percy St, W1 (637–2521). Designs
include Hinkley Point and Didcot power stations, Terminal Buildings at
London Airport and Roman Catholic Cathedral, Liverpool. Current projects
include Great Arundel Court scheme for Capital and Counties, Stock
Conversion hotel on Hyde Park Corner, Coutts Bank in the Strand, and
Regent's Park Mosque.
Projects: **6** 1, **8** 7, **9** 32.

William Holford and Partners, Adelaide House, London Bridge, EC4
(623–5681). Past designs include St Paul's Precinct (1964), and 2nd Piccadilly
scheme (1961).

Sidney Kaye, Eric Firmin and Partners, Thavies Inn House, 5 Holborn
Circus, EC1 (583–8811). Since 1945 have been responsible for nearly 100
major projects in London, including the Hilton Hotel for Charles Clore, Joe
Levy's Euston Centre, the Playboy Club, the Londonderry House Hotel, the
Park Lane Casino, offices for GEC, GKN and Reed Paper Group, ATV House,
synagogues, shopping centres, factories, and the large flats and shopping
complex on south side of Shepherds Bush Green. Kaye has worked closely
with Joe Levy, on Euston Centre, Piccadilly Circus and other schemes.
Projects: **1** 18, **2** 16, **5** 18, **5** 26.

Michael Lyell Associates, 16 Yeomans Row, SW3 (589–7273).
Projects: **2** 41, **5** 32.

Newman Levinson, 9 Mansfield St, W1 (580–9251).
Projects: **5** 14, **6** 3, **6** 19, **10** 12, **10** 17, **1** 26.

Richard Seifert and Partners, 34 Red Lion Square, WC1 (242–1644).
Has had more influence on the London skyline than anyone since Wren.
The company has an annual turnover of more than £50 million, and Seifert
has become a multi-millionaire. b. 1910, son of a doctor; educ. Central
Foundation School and Bartlett; began practice 1934; first major project
Woolworth Ho. 1955. Among his buildings in London in the past ten years
are:

Centre Point, Space House, Drapers Gardens, Inland Revenue block in
Carey Street, London Bridge House, Telstar House, Penta Hotel, Park Tower
Hotel, Royal Garden Hotel, Metropole Hotel, Britannia Hotel, flats in
Kensington Palace Gardens, Dunlop House, St Botolph's House, Westminster
Bank,(Oxford St), International Press Centre, Whittington House, Beagle House,
offices in High Holborn bridging Proctor St, Foster Wheeler House, Guinness
Mahon, Gracechurch St, Kellog House and Univac House. He has also built
offices, hotels and multi-storey car parks in several parts of outer
London, and many other places in Britain and abroad.

He is presently engaged on major projects in all areas of central London
(in addition to a huge 20-acre housing scheme for Wandsworth Council)
including the development of several air termini. Among his other major
projects are the new 600-ft National Westminster block in Bishopsgate, the
Odhams site in Covent Garden, several more big City projects including
Billingsgate Market, Windsor House in Victoria St, the Gamages scheme, the
new offices of *The Times* in Grays Inn Rd, the Imperial War Museum
extension and the Kings Reach scheme in Southwark.
Projects: **2** 9, **4** 1, **4** 20, **4** 26, **5** 2, **5** 5, **5** 23, **6** 3, **6** 10, **6** 20, **7** 14, **8** 3, **8** 9,
9 3, **9** 11, **9** 14, **10** 10, **10** 14, **10** 15, **10** 19, **11** 4, **11** 14, **12** 4, **12** 7, **12** 8,
12 21, **12** 46, **12** 48, **12** 49, **12** 50, **12** 51, **12** 56, **12** 61, **13** 1, **14** 5.

(a)

(b)

(c)

(d)

(e)

a, Richard Seifert; b, Drapers Gardens;
c, Centre Point; d, Space House,
Kingsway; e, Park Tower Hotel,
Knightsbridge.

Planners

A key part is played in any development by the planners. No new building may be erected without planning permission.

All planning applications must go first to the local authority. A successful scheme may go through the following stages:
(1) Informal discussions with the local authority
(2) Formal application for permission
(3) Outline permission granted
(4) Detailed permission granted, on submission of architect's plans
In London the local authorities deal with most applications themselves. But in the case of larger schemes, such as those of more than local significance, railway stations, university buildings, major shopping developments, tower blocks or substantial office or industrial schemes, they seek the direction of the GLC, which is the strategic planning authority for Greater London.

The GLC has also been responsible since 1969 for the Greater London Development Plan, an attempt to co-ordinate London's development and to provide a framework for local planners. It has, for instance, designated 56 'action areas' where redevelopment is to be encouraged in the next ten years.

Plans for most of these will be prepared by local councils, e.g. slum clearance and housing schemes. Others will be undertaken by private developers e.g. plans for office development which is being encouraged on major stations, such as Moorgate and Blackfriars. Others will be initiated by the GLC itself, by the creation of Comprehensive Development Areas, of which Covent Garden is the prototype.

If the GLC turns down a scheme which has been approved by a local authority, it is automatically referred to the DOE for arbitration by the Minister.

Appeals and Public Inquiries

(1) If there is substantial public objection to a proposed scheme *before* planning permission has been granted, the Minister may order a public inquiry.
(2) If the scheme is turned down by the local authority, the *applicant* may appeal to the Minister, This may also result in a public inquiry.
(3) After planning permission has been granted, the public has no further rights. The Minister, however, does have the right to revoke a decision, although this is very rarely exercised, since the local authority then becomes liable to pay compensation, which may run into millions of pounds.

Planning Authorities

In recent years, considerably more public attention has been focused on the elected councillors who govern London — such men as Sir Desmond Plummer, Leader of the GLC, Sir Malby Crofton of Kensington and Chelsea, and Hugh Cubitt, Leader of Westminster City Council. It is these men, and their councils and committees, who take the final planning decisions.

Perhaps even more powerful, however, are the men on whose advice they usually act — the permanent officials; and these men remain largely anonymous.

Camden (Planning Dept, Old Town Hall, High Holborn, WC1 405-3411). Director of Planning and Communications since the Council was formed has been Bruno Schlaffenberg. Camden pursues a more aggressive attitude towards private developers than some councils (e.g. plan for compulsory purchase of Centre Point), and refused to participate in Covent Garden Plan, but has earned opprobrium for some of its extensive housing developments, such as the bleak new Gospel Oak.

Planners

City Corporation (Planning Dept, Guildhall House, 81–7 Gresham St, EC2 606-3030). City Architect and Planning Officer is Edwin Chandler. He played a key part in planning the big office development along Route 11 (South Barbican) and in drawing up the City's strategy for comprehensive redevelopment, including the complex of elevated walk-ways. The City is virtually a planning law unto itself (it remained aloof from the borough re-organisation of 1963), and remains markedly more favourable to new development than any other area.

Royal Borough of Kensington and Chelsea (Planning Dept, Chelsea Town Hall, Kings Road SW3 352-8101). Borough Planning Officer is Charles Hudson. Has generally taken a firm stand over the Borough's extensive conservation areas (he has a good reputation with local amenity societies). Over a number of controversial schemes he has come down heavily on developers, particularly over attempts to slip in offices or hotels in place of residential accommodation, e.g. the corner of Earls Court and Cromwell Rd.

City of Westminster (Planning Dept, City Hall, Victoria St, 828-8070). Director of Architecture and Planning is S. West, and Chief Planning Officer Joe Hirsch. Westminster is the richest local authority in Britain, covers 5,500 acres of central London, including many of the city's best-known and most historic areas, and presents the largest variety of planning problems. The City council has recently been taking a stronger line over certain proposed new developments (e.g. in Wigmore St and Piccadilly), particularly after it drew such strong fire for the Piccadilly Circus scheme in May 1972.

GLC Although the GLC is the strategic planning authority for the 620 square miles of Greater London, its direct powers are few. Even where it has published general directives, as for the amount of new office development, these have not always been respected.

One respect in which the GLC does have considerable impact on the shaping of London is its responsibility for the city's major roads. In 1969 the Greater London Development Plan envisaged the so-called Ringway programme, of three major motorway-type roads ringing London in concentric circles (and involving the demolition of some 30,000 homes), but this proposal has been subject to almost continuous controversy and amendment.

The GLC is also responsible for 570 miles of existing major roads (so-called Metropolitan roads). For many years its engineers have been working to a plan, which originated in the thirties, for road-widening along many parts of this system. This has involved (1) buying up many properties on road frontages, such as the London Pavilion and 1–17 Shaftesbury Avenue; (2) ensuring that 'as and when' redevelopment takes place where road-widening is desired, new buildings are set back. This leaves the old buildings projecting into the street. Such 'as and whens' may be seen in various parts of London (indicating possible redevelopment) e.g. at various points along Brompton Rd and Knightsbridge.

Perhaps the most influential single figure in the planning of London since the War has been Sir Leslie Martin (b. 1908). He was Deputy-Architect to the LCC 1948–53, Chief Architect 1953–6, since when he has been Professor of Architecture at Cambridge. Sir Leslie played a key part in various major plans, including: the Barbican scheme (1959); London University's expansion in Bloomsbury (1959); scheme for the redevelopment of the whole of southern Whitehall (with Buchanan 1965); the moving of Covent Garden Market and consequent Covent Garden Plan (1964–8); National Library scheme (1966–8); Marchmont Development, Brunswick Square.

Sir Leslie also designed the Royal Festival Hall, with Sir Robert Matthew.

Listed Buildings and Conservation Areas

The only buildings which require permission before they can be demolished are those which are listed as being of 'special historical or architectural interest'.

There are in London 13,553 statutory Listed Buildings, and 8,385 on supplementary local lists. These are graded as follows:

Grade I. Buildings of outstanding interest (630)

Grade II. Buildings of special interest (there are some particularly important buildings in this category)

Grade III. Buildings which do not normally qualify for statutory lists, but are important enough to be drawn to the attention of local authorities, so that the case for preserving them can be fully considered.

The full statutory list may be seen at the National Monuments Record, Fortress House, Savile Row, W1. Local lists may be seen at the GLC, or at the appropriate local council office.

How does a building get listed? A recommendation may be made by a member of the public, the local authority or the GLC. All recommendations are made direct to the DOE who, having inspected the building, decide whether it should be listed or not. At present the DOE has only 20 inspectors to cover the whole of Britain.

If someone wishes to demolish a Listed Building, he must apply to the local council for a Listed Building Consent. This must be advertised, and sent to GLC Historic Buildings Division. They pass on their recommendation to the DOE, who take the final decision (possibly after public inquiry).

To protect buildings of special interest which have not yet been listed, local authorities are given the power to serve a Building Preservation Notice. The notice is effective for six months, or until the Minister decides whether or not the building should be listed.

The penalty for demolishing a Listed Building can be an unlimited fine, or imprisonment up to 12 months, or both.

If the owner of a Listed Building fails to take steps to preserve it, or deliberately neglects it in order to redevelop ('encouraged decay'), the local authority has the power to buy it compulsorily. This has so far not happened.

Under the Civic Amenities Act of 1967, all local authorities have been invited to designate Conservation Areas, 'areas of special architectural or historic interest the character or appearance of which is desirable to preserve or enhance'. This does not preclude redevelopment within a Conservation Area, but it is hoped that new buildings will be harmonious with their surroundings, in terms of design and size.

The Role of the Public

If you wish to know about the future of a particular property or site, you may contact 'planning inquiries' at the local authority concerned. They will tell you if a planning application has been made, its nature and the name of the applicant. The staff of most planning offices are very helpful.

If you object to the proposal, you can do one or more of the following things:

The Role of the Public

(1) write stating your reasons for objection to the Borough Planning Officer, the Town Clerk and/or your local Councillor and local MP. There are certain grounds for objection which a planning committee is obliged to consider more seriously than others, e.g. loss of light to surrounding buildings, generation of traffic, overdevelopment of the site, disturbance and extra noise, loss of amenities etc. Objections on grounds of inappropriate architectural treatment are likely to be taken more seriously in a Conservation Area

(2) seek the advice of the local amenity society (the council provide a list of societies on request)

(3) discuss the matter with local residents. A strongly supported petition will ensure that the council take notice

(4) where relevant, seek the advice of a national amenity society e.g. the Georgian Society (2 Chester St, SW1), the Victorian Society (55 Great Ormond St, WC1) or the Society for the Protection of Ancient Buildings (55 Great Ormond St, WC1). It helps to be a member.

(5) if necessary, alert the local newspaper

(6) if you consider a building to be worthy of listing, write to the DOE, setting out its case.

The only time during which a member of the public can have any influence on the future of a scheme is before the council has taken its decision.

Suggestions

1. No building should be allowed to be pulled down without specific permission; i.e. permission to demolish should be simultaneous with planning consent to redevelop.

2. Planning consents should only be valid for two years, instead of five. The present system, under which consents are frequently hoarded, makes it difficult for planners to respond to changes in public opinion, or to keep general control over the tempo of redevelopment.

3. 'Developer's blight' is one of the scandals of present-day London. To prevent buildings being left empty, and allowed to decay, at least rating concessions could be withdrawn, and possibly councils should make more use of their powers of compulsory purchase.

4. Much more attention should be paid to the possibility of refurbishing existing buildings, and finding beneficial new uses for ones which have lost their old function. Councils could do much to encourage this. Buildings which have been *allowed* to decay, inevitably present a much stronger case for demolition (see 3 above).

5. In the changing climate of public opinion, comprehensive schemes such as Piccadilly and Covent Garden, which involve clearance of a large area, have met with increasing disfavour. Planning obviously has an important part to play in co-ordinating redevelopment, but in central London it is rightly becoming hard to justify the demolition of hundreds of buildings to satisfy some large abstract plan.

6. Tenants who have long-standing associations with an area should be given statutory protection, so that a developer must offer them equivalent premises at an 'acceptable' rent. Some of the greatest sufferers from re-development have been shopkeepers, one-room businesses and people living in central, low-rent flats who, after eviction, have found it virtually impossible to find equivalent accommodation. Such people should also be automatically informed of any planning applications relevant to their future (as are landlords).

7. Developers should make a contribution to the large expense incurred by planning procedure, particularly on major schemes.

8. Some reform should be made of the system whereby developers have to be compensated at the full projected value of a development, when planning permission is revoked. The present compensation law is weighted too heavily on the side of the developer. There is one 'loophole' in the law — *where a building has been listed after planning permission has been granted, no compensation is payable.*

9. Too many office redevelopments in London are being pre-let to government departments (e.g. Queen Anne's Mansions, pre-let to the DOE). If developers can make huge profits out of the taxpayer, why should the Government not develop on its own behalf?

10. The ODP system has become a farce, and should either be drastically revised, or abolished.

11. The GLC Historic Buildings Board should be given back the power to list buildings in London which was taken away in 1971. The present division of responsibility with the DOE is time-consuming, anomalous and frustrating to all concerned. The present List, particularly of buildings later than 1840, is very inadequate.

12. The designation of Conservation Areas without adequate listings of those buildings which establish the special character of the area, is an empty exercise.

13. Although on paper the whole planning process is open to public inspection and participation, in practice it still appears to be secretive, complex and mysterious. Much more could still be done to ensure what the planners and councillors insist that they themselves want — i.e. a higher level of public information and participation in the vital early stages. Three suggestions:

(*a*) every council should have available for public inspection a large-scale sheet map showing (1) buildings redeveloped in the past 20 years; (2) buildings on which there are current planning applications; (3) buildings on which the council is engaged in discussions with prospective developers; (4) any road-widening proposals; (5) listed buildings.

(*b*) the GLC (or other bodies) should mount a permanent public exhibition, showing all major proposals, with photographs of existing buildings, and architect's drawings of new ones. Both (*a*) and (*b*) would mean that the public would have no grounds for accusing planning authorities of secrecy. Equally the planners could gain a fuller picture of public reaction.

(*c*) some way should be found to ensure greater participation in public inquiries (at the Covent Garden Inquiry only 18 members of the public turned up in 42 days). All people remotely affected should be directly invited to attend. Possibly on some major schemes a referendum should be held.

(*d*) The Land Registry should be open to free public inspection (as in Scotland) and holdings by nominee companies should be revealed as such.

14. Of all the schemes in this book, we feel that the most unjustifiable is the siting of the new National Library south of the British Museum.